REFLECTIONS ON
LIFE AS A CATHOLIC

REFLECTIONS ON
LIFE AS A CATHOLIC

A Layman's Journey from Innocence to Reality

Richard Emond

Library of Congress Control Number:		2014922064
ISBN:	Hardcover	978-1-5035-2611-2
	Softcover	978-1-5035-2613-6
	eBook	978-1-5035-2612-9

Rev. date: 12/26/2014

To order additional copies of this book, contact:
Xlibris
1-888-795-4274
www.Xlibris.com
Orders@Xlibris.com
701693

CONTENTS

PART SIX: BREAD AND CIRCUSES

PROLOGUE

In a modern Apologia Pro Vita Sua I have attempted to give the rationale for my chronicling of a life that is now in its twilight years. The community of believers is a heterogeneous polyglot to say the least. The New Testament describes them thusly: there are those who receive the word vicariously and quickly fall away. Others receive it with joy but, when temptation comes, fall away. Then there are those who receive the word, digest it, and grow in faith and strength and never falter or look back. For myself I do not fit any of the above situations, but, rather, suggest that there is another category, of which more than a few belong but few would confess to. There is what I would refer to as a "silent majority," if you will, who remain a part of the faithful, attend Mass every Sunday, and consider themselves practicing Catholics. Yet they harbor many reservations as to the dictates of the hierarchy and do not take seriously many of the prohibitions imposed upon them, particularly concerning the matter of birth control. Many choose to follow their informed consciences and rationalize their consequent decisions accordingly. These are often referred to by the hierarchy as "cafeteria Catholics," a pejorative appellation in current vogue. Actually I've had some very good meals in cafeterias and find the label offensive and judgemental. These individuals reject the "one size fits all" approach that the Church finds so convenient to adopt.

Much reflection on my life as a Catholic has brought me to the depressing conclusion that the religion is more form than substance. For example, in the New Testament, are the words of Jesus what he actually said or are they what others, the evangelists, to be precise, say that he said? Events described as miracles, for instance, the raising of Lazarus, could have a natural explanation. Might he have merely been in a coma? Much is shrouded in the ancient mists of time and cannot be definitively proven one way or the other. There are those who even question whether Jesus really existed at all or, if he did, was he really God or merely another prophet. It is not my objective to explore such matters but merely to raise the point that more seems to be based on faith rather than objective, tangible evidence. It appears unlikely, after the passage of more than two centuries, that anything will surface to definitively prove or disprove the story as promulgated by the Catholic Church.

My lifelong close association with Catholicism makes it impossible for me to view it in a completely detached, objective manor. Its emotional roots are deep and impossible for me to uproot. I find myself in a state of suspended animation, as it were, not able to completely refute what I have absorbed from my faith, yet not able to completely accept it either. What I find most disturbing are the attacks on the Church by some very prominent theologians, such as Schillebeeckx, Rahner, Kung, and Curran. Some would counter this with the shibboleth that you can be too smart for your own good. While, admittedly, this may be true, I would counter that it is also possible, if not more so, to be too stupid for your own good. Yet, when all is said and done, the so-called "liberal" faction of the Church, as opposed to the "conservative" side, appears to have a corner on the market when it comes to intellectual heavy lifting. This should be, at minimum, a cause for concern to the faithful.

My purpose in writing has been two-fold. Firstly, I wish to leave behind a legacy for those nearest and dearest to me, giving a chronicle of events as I saw them and how I subsequently reacted. There is no purpose of evasion or intent to impute guilt on anyone, only the desire to set the record straight, if you will, as only one in the first-person status can do. Secondly, I wanted to critique the shortcomings which I came to experience along the way, while still trying to remain faithful to the Church as best my conscience would permit. Trying to be constructively critical, I have detailed what can be easily verified by all who wish to cast a watchful eye on current events as reported by, I would submit, a mostly unbiased media, not only the secular but the religious press. As to the former, the Washington Post, the Boston Globe, and the New York Times deserve mention and, as to the latter, the National Catholic Reporter stands out. I have, unfortunately, found the Catholic Church to be much more concerned about its reputation and survival than the welfare of its flock, as illustrated notably in the Holocaust and the sex abuse scandal. If it had been nearly as concerned for the welfare of its "born" as it has been for the "unborn," we would all be a lot better off.

One of the modern problems the Catholic Church has had to face is the increased longevity of its members. Until at least fifty years ago, the faithful could be more readily accepting of the promise of a future happy existence in the afterlife following what was for many a not particularly serendipitous one on earth. In times past many died young of incurable diseases, while others worked long and hard just to survive, many dying before retirement and others not long thereafter. A belief in a blessed afterlife was all that many had to hold on to. Now, with people living longer, they are demanding more material pleasures in the here and now in addition to what spiritual pleasures might be waiting beyond the grave. This has, I submit, presented a new challenge for the Church and one which it has not contended with particularly well. The matters of artificial insemination, birth control, marriage and divorce come quickly to mind. People are no longer content, nor should they be, with the proposition that they should be miserable here below in order to be happy in the next life.

The Catholic Church in the modern world finds that it no longer has a monopoly on higher education or religious education, for that matter. Many laymen as well as lay women are not only as well educated, but even better educated, than the clergy and are no longer content to be led as though they were Shropshire sheep. They want a place at the table, so to speak, and, thanks largely to Vatican II, are getting it. There is no going back now and the old order must give way to the new. The rebirth of the order of the lay deacon was a good start and, hopefully, the order of deaconesses will not be far behind. Who would have thought, before Vatican II, that there would be altar girls as well as altar boys? There are cracks now in the glass ceiling even of the Roman Catholic Church.

The Church in the time of Christ was inevitably influenced by the mores of the age in which it lived. Surely Christ's choice of an all-male discipleship was in line with the Jewish practice then in vogue. To attempt to carry this over to today's church by insisting on an all-male clergy is not only farcical but out of sync with contemporary mores. Contrariwise, celibacy was not a requirement for discipleship whereas it is insisted upon today. With no basis in scripture, but only in tradition, both of these supposed pillars of Catholicism could be brought down overnight with the concurrence of the Pope, but don't hold your breath waiting for that to happen. Unless the Church more readily adapts itself to the society in which it lives, it will not continue, after another generation, to exist as we now know it. Its geopolitical center has already moved from Europe and is now seeking foundations in Africa and Asia, a Sisyphean endeavor I would suggest. The Roman Catholic Church reached the apex of its religious and political power in the Middle Ages and has been in decline since at least the middle of the nineteenth century. This realization actually prompted the convening of Vatican I, when the doctrine of papal infallibility was needlessly proclaimed.

My fondest desire is that what I have written will be accepted for what it truly is: a desire to share my religious journey from the vantage point of one best qualified to assess it, both subjectively and, hopefully, objectively. It is a journey I would not have wanted to miss for anything in this world or, for that matter, in the next.

PART ONE

In the Beginning

CHAPTER 1

A Tentative Start

My untimely arrival on the afternoon Thursday, June 22, 1939, along with that of my twin brother, I being the younger by about ten minutes, did not bode well. Being about seven weeks premature, it was seriously thought that neither of us would survive. Although the odds on me were a tad better than those on my twin, they were hovering around the 50-50 mark. While such a situation would not be considered in the least problematic today, one has to remember that this was 1939 and medicine was not nearly as advanced as it is today. We were placed in incubators and, I believe, remained in them for about three or four weeks. As our condition was touch-and-go my mother thought it wise to call for a priest to administer Baptism should we not make it out of the hospital. However, the priest, for whatever reason, decided that this was not necessary, and refused to administer the sacrament. According to Catholic theology at the time any child dying without Baptism would be consigned to Limbo, a murky place that was neither Heaven nor Hell. Church theology has since given up on this notion and consigned Limbo to limbo, if you will, affirming that God's eternal mercy will save the unbaptized after all.

As a result of all this, my father, who was not particularly religiously inclined, took such umbrage at the priest that he resolved that we wouldn't be baptized at all. My mother, however, being more faithful to Church orthodoxy, was determined that we would be baptized at the earliest possible time. Apparently afraid to risk the wrath of my father and due to our still relatively frail physical development, and not wanting to venture out with us during the cold Winter months, the opportunity to have this sacrament performed did not present itself until about nine months after we were born. Even then, my mother, while my father was at work, took us and her sister-in-law to the church to have the ceremony performed. A somewhat humorous encounter ensued. The church secretary asked how old we were and, instead of answering forthrightly, my aunt said we were two months premature, which, if course, wasn't an answer at all. When asked again, she simply repeated the mantra, but I'm sure the real truth eventually had to be divulged. After all, we were able to walk to our own baptism, something which few cradle Catholics are able to say. Now, thank God, we were finally saved from Limbo. While both fathers, my father and "father" were wrong in this matter, I believe my spiritual father bears the brunt of the blame. We should have been given the benefit of the doubt and been baptized in case either one of us or both should have eventually died. If I were the priest I wouldn't have wanted to have that on my conscience.

If it weren't for my mother, I'm sure that we wouldn't have been brought to church at all as my father was, to say the least, not what one would describe as a devout Catholic. He apparently once remarked that he would conform to Catholic regulations that we be brought up Catholic but, when we were old enough to know our own minds, we could then decide what we wanted to do. As is not unusual in a family, where there is disagreement between the parents on religious matters, the mother generally has the upper hand. Our religious roots came from French-Irish ancestors on both my father's and my mother's side, my father's father being French and his mother being Irish and the same scenario prevailing in my mother's ancestry. Not being Catholic was hardly an option.

In a somewhat unusual situation, we attended a church that was at least three miles from our home and outside the official boundaries of that church, Corpus Christi, even though we were only a mile from another church, St. Ambrose, whose boundaries included our address. Catholic churches have strict boundaries establishing who should be considered parishoners in their respective parishes. These parishoners are then expected to register with that particular parish. This way the church can keep tabs on them and know where to send envelopes for their weekly contributions, among other things. Also, in the cases of sickness and or imminent death, the church member has a right to call upon the respective clergy for their ministrations. It makes for an orderly administration of their services.

While growing up, I was almost always in attendance at Corpus Christi, which was reachable more conveniently by public transportation, than at St. Ambrose, which was within easy walking distance. I remember a few occasions when my grandmother on my mother's side, in whose house we lived, took me to church on Sunday and it was always to St. Ambrose as she didn't have access to a car and couldn't drive anyway. I don't recall her ever attending Corpus Christi. When she would go to church without me, people would ask, "where is your little boy?" Who says a house divided against itself cannot stand? One of the more memorable sermons given by the pastor, a Monsignor Mason, was a plaintive plea by him for help by the congregation to help find his pet, "Dickie-Bird" Mason, which had gone missing. I don't recall if it was ever found. Looking back, I surmise that my affiliation with Corpus Christi was predicated on my mother's early and middle childhood. My grandfather on my mother's side owned a small grocery which was nearer Corpus Christi. Since he could drive and my grandmother couldn't, I suspect that my mother was put in their school as he could easily drop her off and pick her up afterwards. She could then spend time with him at his store until it was time to close up shop.

One of my more memorable impressions of Sundays at Mass was the taking of the collection just before the Offertory. Unlike now, the basket was passed by the priests themselves. Talk about intimidation. Those who gave generously got an approving smile from Father, not to mention a notation in the weekly bulletin. My father did not always accompany us to church, my parents having separated when I was two years old, and one of the regular parishoners, a portly woman whom my father referred to as "big Mary," would ask my mother, "where is your husband?" Such was life in the '40's and '50's.

Corpus Christi was, at the time, a thriving downtown parish, being not far from the central shopping district of Rochester, N.Y. It also benefited from the families of students attending its grammar school. It was considered a "plum" assignment for clergy hoping to go on to bigger and better things, whether it be an assignment as secretary to the bishop or, in fact, the bishopric itself. During my early years there the pastor, in fact, was Vicar General of the diocese, a position at the time second only to the bishop himself. The church had a long and glorious history indeed. When it came time, however, for me to start grade school, I did not attend the parochial school at Corpus Christi, being sent instead to a private Catholic school, Nazareth Hall, which was a least another five miles away. We were chauffered there in a private limousine, which picked us up and dropped us off after school. This was done because my mother had to work 40 hours a week and it would have been a chore for my grandmother to accompany us by bus to and from school. The driver, William Siegfried, was a real no nonsense, cigar smoking type of guy. We were picked up promptly at home and brought back as soon as school ended. I never knew how much it cost my mother for the convenience of a private school but am sure it didn't come cheap. As there was no help from my father she had to bear the entire burden herself.

I still remember my first grade teacher, Sister Agnes Cecilia, who, incidentally, died just a few years ago, a nun of the order of St. Joseph and quickly learned that what they said was law, absolute and unquestioning. These sisters to me were bigger than life and would make the Nazi Gestapo seem like wimps. I couldn't imagine these individuals performing acts that we mere mortals took for granted. In these pre-Vatican II days they wore cumbersome clothing, all black, except for a white bib in front and a partial white covering around the face, the hair and ears never being exposed. These women, though not deeply immersed in academia, were, nonetheless, totally committed to their mission. I still admire them as I have admired few other people in my life. Having chosen the sisterhood as their vocation they pursued it with gusto and never looked back. They lived a rather cloistered life, not even being allowed to travel by themselves, having always to go in pairs. Their lives, in stark contrast to those of the priest, were literally quite circumscribed and cloistered. These nuns were a sort of surrogate mother as I spent more time with them than I did with my biological mother, who, unfortunately, had to work full time at the Eastman Kodak Compnay downtown. They made a most lasting impression on me, one which, I dare say, I feel the effects of even to this present time. Their influence in my upbringing cannot be overstated.

I have little, if any, recollection of my life prior to my sixth birthday, which occurred just a few months before my entering grammar school. Back then kindergarten was not considered a vital educational requirement. I have heard it proclaimed by modern educators that the lack of early childhood education, not only kindergarten but pre-kindergarten, renders one socially handicapped for a lifetime. I find this to be questionable and look askance at today's propensity to put children into school almost from the time they are able to walk. Socialization is definitely the buzzword of the times. Many of today's children probably cannot remember a time when they were not in school. A dubious legacy, I would submit.

I led what would be referred to today as a "sheltered" existence, safe within the cocoon of my family and that of the Catholic school. My playmates were my own siblings, primarily my twin brother. In those days twins were dressed alike and were encouraged to stay together. I remember the guessing games people engaged in, trying to determine which was which. We were always referred to as a pair, "the twins," rather than as separate individuals. Twinship is undeniably a unique relationship. Regardless of our success, or lack of it, with respect to relations with others, we always had each other. We even thought alike and, for the most part, still do to this present day. Twins were not nearly as common when we were born as they are today. Supposedly twins skip generations, and, in fact, my paternal grandfather was a twin. According to this theory I should then have twin grandchildren, and so on and so on. It is also theorized that twins are invariably left-handed and, in our case, that was also true. This being the era before it was considered necessary to correct what was then thought to be a biological aberration, no attempt was made to force us to use our right hand. Since supposedly only ten percent of the population is left-handed, I am a distinct minority within a religious minority. I take umbrage at my culture which disparages the left, as in the criticism of one as being "out in left field." Then there is the reference to one's trusted associate as being "one's right-hand man." Be that as it may, lest this screed devolve into a study of linguistics, it is time to move on.

CHAPTER 2

Total Immersion

My first day of school in the first grade was a memorable, if not traumatic, one indeed. Here I was in the total care of the Sisters of St. Joseph at Nazareth Hall, a private Catholic school for boys only. Little did I know then that I would attend boys-only schools for 17 of the next 20 years of my educational formation. Although forced by financial resources, or, should I say, a lack thereof, Catholic schools have been forced to turn to co-ed education with increasing frequency. However, modern educational theory has tended to validate the maxim that the sexes learn better when taught apart from each other. Having no sister as a sibling, I did not find the environment strange or uncomfortable.

Our textbook was the Baltimore Catechism, No.2, which, I believe, has its roots as far back as the Council of Trent in 1545. The format was one of questions and answers, many of which were to be memorized and recited by rote at the teacher's command. I can never forget the first question and its corresponding answer. Why did God make me? God made me to know, love, and serve him in this world and to be happy with him in the next. This pretty much seemed to sum it all up and who could argue with that? The Catechism was divided into various parts, detailing such matters as what constituted a venial or mortal sin with accompanying illustrations, what were the seven sacraments, etc. It was all very neat, orderly, and reassuring. The whole purpose of life and how to attain it was all there in a nutshell, so to speak.

As most of my day was spent under the tutelage of the nuns, it is most undeniable that they had a very profound and lasting influence on my character formation. How could it have been otherwise? I sometimes joke that they made me what I am today, whatever that is. If nothing else, although there was much else, they taught me discipline and respect for authority. These twin attributes go a long way in keeping one on the straight and narrow so as to avoid falling into what was then, and still is, often referred to by the Church as the ways of the wicked world.

It seemed to me then, as it would for a long time afterward, that the Catholic Church had the answer to any problem, real or imagined. This certainty was reinforced regularly by the nuns and, occasionally, by the priests, who would visit on special occasions. There was always high anticipation when "Father" was going to speak to the class. In my case that priest was Father Randall, who, sometime after, was elevated to the rank of Monsignor, an honor bestowed on those who have in some way distinguished themselves in the service of the Church. Both the nuns and the priests were bigger than life figures in my mind and would remain so throughout my formative years.

The second watershed, the first being Baptism, in my Catholic upbringing was the reception of Holy Communion, which, I believe, I received on Mother's Day in 1947. I once had a certificate attesting to it but that has since gotten lost in the various moves one encounters along life's journey.

One of the prerequisites for First Holy Communion was the reception of the sacrament of Penance, now, post-Vatican II, more properly referred to as Reconciliation. The confessional box was that dark, secret place where you poured out your soul to Father, who would then give absolution, in Latin of course, and then have you say for your penance something along the lines of three Our Fathers and three Hail Marys. I did not know it then but, throughout the course of my life, the sacrament of Penance, sometimes also referred to as Confession, would become an integral part of my spiritual life, being the recipient of it an untold number of times. It is in fact only one of four sacraments that can be received more than once, the others being Matrimony, Holy Communion, and the Anointing of the Sick, which, pre-Vatican II, was called Extreme Unction. I remember the long lines at confessionals on Saturday night, presumably to obtain the remission of sin in time to receive Holy Communion on Sunday. A practice I developed early for reception of the sacrament, as prescribed by my teachers, was to recite a "laundry list" of sins, including how many times they were committed, and asking for God's forgiveness.

There was a veritable plethora of sins one could commit, some deemed worthy of eternal damnation, so I never had difficulty in obtaining material worthy of a good confession.

Penance, as it was then, and is still sometimes called, was often linked to the ritual of a Saturday night bath, wherein, one having been cleansed both bodily and spiritually, was made worthy of receiving the body and blood of Christ the following day.

I had now received the first three of the seven sacraments of the Roman Catholic Church. The next in progression would be Confirmation, which I received at the age of twelve. This sacrament harks back to the event called Pentecost, when the twelve apostles and Mary, the Mother of God, were enlivened by the Holy Spirit ten days after the ascension of Christ. A sponsor is required for the reception of this sacrament and this individual, of course, must be a Catholic of good standing. That person accompanies the one to be confirmed to the church and places his or her hand on the recipient's left shoulder as the sacrament is administered by the local bishop. In the case of an adult, the sacrament may be administered by the parish priest, as is usually done during the Easter Vigil Mass. These individuals, usually non-Catholics, will have had to have gone through a lengthy learning process referred to as RCIA, the Rite of Christian Initiation of Adults. However, I digress. My sponsor for Confirmation was a great uncle, he having married my paternal grandfather's sister. Upon being confirmed I was to be imbued with the seven gifts of the Holy Spirit, then referred to as the Holy Ghost. These, are, to wit, Wisdom, Understanding, Counsel, Fortitude, Knowledge, Piety, and Fear of the Lord. This was only so much gobbledegook to me at the time and, I can honestly say, isn't even all that illuminating to me even now. Be that as it may, I was now considered a "soldier of Christ," part of the Church militant here on earth, the other two parts of the Church being the Church suffering, those in Purgatory, and the Church triumphant, those in Heaven. I wondered if it were possible for one to receive all seven sacraments of the Church and, although rare, it is indeed possible. This relates to the reception of the sacraments of Matrimony and Holy Orders. Since priests are obliged to be celibate, both these sacraments could nonetheless be received if a man, after becoming a widower, decided to enter the priesthood. I personally don't know anyone who would fit that description. In any event, such individuals are rare indeed. The closest approximation to it in today's church would be deacons who never receive the full order of priesthood. They may be married when ordained as deacons but, should they become widowers, they are not allowed to remarry. I could expect to receive two more sacraments in my life- time, although neither would be considered as necessary for my salvation as the previous four.

There I was, still only eleven years old, and it seemed that my salvation game plan was very much in order. Little did I know what still lay before me. I was now in the fifth grade of elementary school but had not already been trained to be an altar boy at my parish church of Corpus Christi. That would come later when I entered eighth grade at Corpus Christi's parochial school. This would be a brief interlude in my private schooling, which would pick up again immediately after, but more of that later. One incident, which occurred in the sixth grade, traumatic as it was, still stands indelibly etched in my memory. During a lesson given by the teacher, which I was then expected to replicate in class, I failed to understand the gist. However, observing that the rest of the class seemed to comprehend and was performing the follow-up task successfully, I was fearful of admitting I couldn't comply. The nun, upon realizing my inactivity, came to my desk and slapped me so forcefully, that the imprint was left for sometime afterward. I later recounted to my mother what had happened and she henceforth went to the principal and complained that she wasn't paying good money to have me slapped around. She was then assured that this would not happen again and the nun was called in and reprimanded. In the meantime, as I advanced through elementary school, the commandments and dictates of the Church were firmly implanted in my mind. I was constantly reminded that I had to avoid the sins lurking around me which were the trademarks of the corruption of the world. What was impressed upon me early on was the distinction between the two types of sins, to wit, mortal and venial. Venial sins, such as disobeying your parents, were offenses against God's infinite love, but did not constitute matter serious enough to send one to Hell and everlasting damnation. Mortal sins, however, would do just that and were to be avoided at all cost. There was a whole plethora of sins of this sort, many being of a sexual nature, such as adultery or fornication. The Church, it seems, has always had an obsession with sins of a sexual content. The lists of such sins have actually undergone revision over the years but still remain somewhat cumbersome and are frequently referred to as "laundry lists" of sins. A good Catholic must know not only the ten commandments but the various sins contained under each commandment. I lived in almost daily fear of committing any sin that might send me on a straight path to Hell, as it seemed, according to the nuns, that mortal sin was all around me. We were assured, however, that no accumulation of venial sins ever equaled a mortal sin. They were to be avoided, nonetheless, as they weakened one's resistance to mortal sin. Of course there was always confession should I succumb to temptation. I could then start all over again with a clean slate.

Growing up Catholic was not easy as, even outside the cocoon of the church and school, it was advised not to socialize with those of other faiths lest one be contaminated with their erroneous beliefs. Apparently the Catholic way was, if not the only way to salvation, certainly by far the best. I never had any contact with Protestants or Jews. One of our neighbors was a Protestant family and relations with them were strained. The husband and wife were not hesitant to voice their anti-Catholic views, thus reinforcing on my impressionable mind that they truly were the enemy after all. I remember the wife always tossing around that old chestnut about the corrupt popes during the Middle Ages. I remember thinking that if she had to reach that far back for something to smear the Church with then the Church couldn't really be so bad after all.

An abrupt change was about to occur in my Catholic upbringing as will be described in the next chapter. Its influence would be momentarily meaningful but, in the final event, not long-lasting.

PART TWO

Into the Maelstrom

CHAPTER 3

Eighth Grade – A Brief Co-Ed Interlude

Little did I know that my grammar school education at Nazareth Hall was to be summarily ended when I finished the seventh grade. I had every expectation of graduating from the academy as my older brother had done just two years before. What transpired came as a complete surprise not only to my family but, I am sure, to all the other students and parents. An announcement was made at a meeting of teachers and parents that, beginning with the next academic year, the school would be converted into a military academy with the students now being cadets. Reaction to this was swift and, if I recollect correctly, somewhat negative. I believe that the individual who gave the presentation was the leader of a local ROTC outfit. My mother was dead set against this and resolved then and there to discontinue my and my twin brother's education at Nazareth Hall and to put us into parochial school at Corpus Christi, our home parish. She had never intended to send us to a military academy and wasn't about to start now. Moreover, the cost of uniforms and other paraphernalia that might be required was an additional expense she surely didn't need. Thus began our co-ed education away from a boys-only private school.

Having been in the sheltered cocoon of a private school for seven years, I admittedly entered this new environment with a bit of trepidation and apprehension. This was, however, soon assuaged by my eighth grade teacher, Sister Gervase, a nun of the order of St. Joseph, not unlike those I had at Nazareth Hall. Ironically, like me, she was a twin and that sister was also a nun, named Protase. I had always assumed that their names honored female saints but, strangely enough, this was not the case. Their namesakes were Gervasius and Protasius, two male saints from the second century who were both martyred under the Roman Emperor Nero. Apparently the names were given a feminine inculturation as "Gervase" and "Protase" and used by women religious. I don't know of a similar incidence of this in Catholic hagiography, possibly because there wasn't any.

Sister Gervase was of a radiantly outgoing nature and seemed to take a "shine" to me and my brother. Possibly this was because we were also twins but, beyond that, I believe, it was attributable to her discovering that we were going to the minor seminary to study for the priesthood upon graduating from grammar school. In that regard, I had a preference to attend a private boys high school, Aquinas, rather than going to the seminary. Aquinas, whose namesake was St. Thomas Aquinas, had a solid academic and athletic reputation, being administered and staffed by the Basilian Fathers, headquartered in Canada. However this was a decision totally out of my control. Aquinas was a good bit more expensive than St. Andrew's, which was the minor seminary. Ironically enough I would later attend a Basilian institution anyway, but more of that later. My mother, being financially constrained, and, getting no help from my father, wouldn't entertain any other option. Many years later, when I saw my father for the last time, he would claim that he did not agree with our being sent to the seminary, but did nothing financially to make any other outcome feasible. My twin brother, because of his more passive nature, I assume, was more resigned to this decision. I, to the contrary, only grudgingly accepted it. However, I am getting ahead of myself. Sister Gervase, far and away, was my favorite teacher in grammar school and I harbor fond memories of her.

As was inevitable, I suppose, word got around that we had come from a private boys school and there was some girlish teasing as a result. Not unsurprisingly no meaningful relationship of a girl nature developed during that year if, in fact, any relationship at that stage of development can truly be called meaningful. I remember being teased to ask one particular girl to go out with me and, after working up the sufficient courage, I did just that and she summarily declined. No further attempts were made with her or, for that matter, with anyone else.

I remember that we went home for lunch, as the school was only about three miles away. Also, on occasion, my grandmother would accompany us back to school on the bus. Oftentimes we walked home after school as there was no deadline to be met and, as mentioned previously, it was only three miles away. It was also during this time that I received my training as an altar boy. Back then, in what seems like ages ago, the Mass was said in

Latin. I had to dutifully memorize my parts in response to what the priest said, also in Latin, of course. Introibo ad altare Dei (I will go to the altar of God), Qui laetificat ad juventutem meam (who gives joy to my youth), etc., etc. Latin was to continue to be the official language of the Church until more than twenty years later, when, as prescribed by Vatican II, it was permitted to say Mass in the vernacular. I must admit that I liked the Latin as it had a certain majesty about it and wasn't vulgar as was the language of the street. Also I could go to Mass anywhere in the world and the language would be the same, not that I was going anywhere anytime soon. The missals were published giving Latin and it's English equivalent side by side so it was easy enough to follow along. Also, the hymns had a certain bigger than life aspect which they lose when translated into the vernacular. In those days there were also High and Low Masses, the former being more grandiose with more candles, more singing, and the burning of incense. Latin also reached it's apogee during such services. At that time no foreign languages were taught at the grammar school level, so it wouldn't be until my first year of high school that I was academically introduced to Latin.

For some reason, still unbeknownst to me, I faltered in my academic performance while my twin brother excelled me. I struggled to get through the first semester, doing poorly particularly in math, which has always been my bête-noire, with science running a close second. Then there was the "hardship" of not being chauffered back and forth to school and having to mingle with the "rabble" that attended parochial school. My spiritual training went on apace, nonetheless, as the parish church was only a few yards away from the school. There was also a certain added security in the person of one of the parish priests who was assigned to Corpus Christi the year he was ordained which, incidentally, just happened to be the year I was born. In the event, he remained there for nineteen years, a situation which would rarely be repeated today, as an attempt is now made to keep rotations more circumscribed, for the benefit supposedly of both clergy and the faithful. This was the priest I regularly confessed to on Saturday night and often wonder if he didn't get tired of hearing the same old laundry list of sins week after week. Other clergy would come and go but he was always there. It also just happened that a cousin of his, who would eventually go to the seminary as well, had graduated from Nazareth Hall two years earlier.

After struggling through my first semester, I attained a firmer grasp of my studies and proceeded to "make the grade," so to speak. I was determined to finish grammar school with the proficiency and discipline that was to be expected from one attending a Catholic school and, ultimately, I succeeded.

I remember well the graduation ceremony as it was my first, but, by far, not the last commencement exercise I would be involved in. There was a visiting priest in the parish at that time, who was a member of the Holy Ghost Fathers, an order whose mission was, among other things, to train seminarians for the priesthood. I remember him, aware that my brother and I were entering the seminary, commenting that the parish was not entering enough candidates for the priesthood into the seminary. To the best of my recollection only two candidates for the priesthood were in their final training and would soon be ordained. I have no idea how many years it had been since others were ordained from the parish. Little did he know that even my brother and I were not entering because of what is familiarly referred to as a "calling" to the priesthood, but, rather, due to financial issues in furthering our continued Catholic education. How many others might be following the same path for the same reason is anybody's guess, although I can be reasonably sure we were not the only ones.

As the first stage of my Catholic education came to an end, I could now look forward to returning to the educational genre I had been immersed in the first seven years of schooling, that of a private boys school. Even during my brief experience of co-ed education, my life outside the classroom did not significantly change. My outside circle of friends was exclusively with other boys, which, I submit, is not all that unusual for a pre-teen male. Also, in the final analysis, there was always the companionship of my twin brother. We played baseball, went to the movies, attended birthday parties with neighbors' children, all of this being carefully monitored by my grandmother in whose house we lived. Sometimes we played in the street or, preferably, organized games of baseball at a nearby park. Being only fourteen years old it wasn't possible to get a work permit as the minimum age was eighteen. I would have two more carefree Summers of reading and playing before entering the world of work as a golf caddy, which didn't require a permit. In the meantime there were vacations to be anticipated and enjoyed.

I often look back on the fifties as a good time to be growing up and, as I reflect on those years, I am truly convinced that it was. Call it the "Happy Days" syndrome if you will, but I view it as much more than nostalgia. Sometimes what are referred to as the "good old days" really were good old days.

My passing from the parochial school after eighth grade to begin my first year of high school would ordinarily be seen as a "bridge" between one environment and a new one, but, in my case, it took on more the character of an "interregnum". I was, in effect, reverting to my past history of single sex education after a very brief hiatus. The only significant difference now was that, instead of being taught only by nuns, I would now be taught exclusively by priests. This was a pattern that would continue throughout my academic career, as I would rarely again have a female instructor, even when I attended Catholic and secular schools after my seminary life was over.

My Catholic foundations, formed early and strong, were to be solidified even more in the years ahead. What had gone before was to be only a foretaste of what was to follow. The maelstrom awaited.

Chapter 4

Minor Seminary - Years of Formation

When I entered high school at St. Andrew's, the minor seminary in Rochester, this event would mark the first time I attended school outside the city limits and, as circumstances would play out, the furthest I would ever travel to attend school. St. Andrew's was about seven and a half miles from home and required three individual trips by public transportation to get there. This was occasioned by the fact that I had to first take a city bus to Corpus Christi church to attend morning Mass. Then it was necessary to take another bus to the local Trailways terminal in order to reach the seminary, which, being in the suburban town of Gates, wasn't serviced by city bus. The ultimate destination of the Trailways was Buffalo, the school being, appropriately enough, situated on what was referred to as "the Buffalo Road." The return trip was abridged a bit since, after being transported back to Trailways, I had to connect with only one bus to get home, there being no need to stop again at church.

There wasn't a day that passed without my having to be in church. During the school week the day started with my going to Mass at my parish church, Corpus Christi, after which I commuted to the seminary. On Saturday, while not required to go to Mass, I did have to go to confession in the evening, this being a weekly obligation imposed on seminarians. There were four priests assigned to the church but I always went to the same one, Father McVeigh, who was in the confessional on the left side at the back of the church. This being pre-Vatican II, you never confessed face-to-face but, rather, always knelt behind the screen which hid your identity. However I am sure the priest could surmise who I was as he knew I had to go to weekly confession and heard the same laundry list of sins week after week. Also he would see me after confession as it was necessary afterwards to ensure that everything in the pews was in order for Sunday and we visited in the sacristy with the sacristan, Beatrice Kerwin, who saw that the altar vestments and the altar were properly set up for Sunday. It was rumored that she had wanted to be a nun but, due to a physical handicap, was not allowed to enter the sisterhood. Then, of course, there was the obligatory attendance at Mass on Sunday, which applied to all Catholics, not just seminarians.

During the '50's, the Catholic Church was thriving and the parish garnered at least five hundred dollars in Sunday collections, a not inconsiderable sum for those days. Masses were well attended and there was what was then called a High Mass at 11 o'clock. This was distinguished from the more common Low Mass by choir singing, more candles being lit, incense being burned, etc. It was at least fifteen minutes longer than the other Masses. This was the Mass we were expected to attend, garbed in proper attire, such as cassock and surplus, making us readily identifiable as students for the priesthood. The rest of the day was taken up partly with finishing up any studies necessary to be ready for the following week. Going to the movies was a welcome diversion as there were local movie houses back then, which were even within walking distance.

At St. Andrew's my favorite class in my first year was Latin, which was taught by Father Gibbons, a roly-poly, ruddy-faced man with a somewhat short temper. Even though many students found Latin a continuing struggle, I took to it like a duck to water. If Father Gibbons was having trouble getting answers to some questions, he zeroed in on me as he knew I always had the answer. I didn't mind being singled out even though I suppose I could be referred to pejoratively as "the teacher's pet." Other teachers of note remain forever etched in my memory. Father Shamon, who taught English, was far and away the best English teacher I ever had. He was brimming with energy and gave his classes the maximum input in the allotted period of time. I attribute to him my excellent grasp of English grammar and spelling. Father Quinn was my History and French teacher, also very skilled in his subject matters. The History courses dwelt on Western European and American backgrounds. Then there was Father Lynch, a rather brilliant teacher of Science, a subject, along with Math, which were my bête-noires. My strong points were, and always remained, History and Language. Finally there was Father Murley, who taught Mathematics, including Algebra and Geometry. This being a seminary, the classes were relatively small, comprising, I would estimate, no more than 15-20 students and discipline was well maintained, making for an optimal learning environment.

If it is true that an institution gets a lot of its environment from the top then, on reflection, I would submit that this was not positive for St. Andrew's. In 1951, the then rector, a Monsignor Lyons, an apparently fatherly-like and approachable individual, died suddenly of a heart attack. and was replaced by a Monsignor Connell, who was quite the opposite. Unfortunately a position such as this was not necessarily filled depending on one's qualifications but, rather, on one's, shall I say, political connections in the old boys network. Apparently Monsignor Connell, a rather austere individual, had the connections and got what was considered a "plum" assignment. Most notably I remember one traumatic incident. One of the students, while in the lunch line, said to the kitchen help, "what slop is on the menu today?" or words to that effect. This was subsequently reported and the rector then ordered the offender to apologize to the kitchen worker in the cafeteria in front of the entire student body. The student was then expelled from the seminary anyway and, I understand, subsequently left the church. Surely this could have and should have been handled in a more understanding and humane manner. This was, however, not Monsignor Connell's style. When Connell later left to accept another "plum" assignment at a flourishing parish, he was subsequently replaced by one of the faculty, Father Quinn, who was well-connected with the diocesan hierarchy, a well-meaning, perhaps, but not especially touchy-feely person.

I spent at least two hours a night on homework so, during the week, there was limited time to watch tv. That caused me to look forward with even more anticipation to the weekend when I could stay up and watch some favorite shows, some of which were "I Remember Mama," and "The Life of Riley" on Friday nights. Later I took a keen interest in the Friday night fights sponsored by Gillette, which then even included championship fights, well before the era of HBO. Then on Saturday night there was the "Jackie Gleason Show", and on Sunday "The 64,000 Question", which, by today's standards, would seem like small potatoes compared to such shows as "Who Wants To Be a Millionaire?" But then you have to remember this was back in the '50's.

My freshman year passed rather uneventfully and the following Summer of '54 was to be the last work-free one I would experience. I remember doing a lot of reading over that Summer, a habit which I picked up from my mother and which I have retained over the ensuing years. Books have been a great source of pleasure to me throughout my life and I haunted the local library which was within walking distance of the house. My preferences have always been history and biography, only rarely picking up a novel other than those I had to read as part of a class assignment.

I continued to do well with my studies in my sophomore year but this was a watershed of sorts as my twin brother fell behind, particularly not having a firm grasp of Geometry. He had to repeat the sophomore year the following Fall and this marked the first time he and I were not together in class since starting grade school. It was surmised that my excelling him in some subjects was intimidating and that our being separated would be beneficial to him. Thus I would begin my junior year while he was still a sophomore.

Haven gotten by Algebra and Geometry I found my third year to be less stressful. I advanced in Latin with the subject matter being the orations of Cicero. Also my French continued apace as well as my History classes. Meanwhile English was enlivened with the study of the works of Shakespeare. My education was a well-rounded one in what was referred to as the "Liberal Arts." This type of education, frowned on by many today, teaches one how to live rather than how to make a living. It is in a very real way it's own reward and I consider it invaluable for its own sake. There is certainly time later in college to specialize in a particular field with the intention of making a living from it. A background in Liberal Arts is, I submit, a perfect foundation.

My Senior year, and the final one for high school, proved the most challenging. In order to graduate one had to take what were the Regents exams, instituted by the State of New York. One drawback here was that one was tempted to study for the test itself rather than the subject matter as a whole. It just so happened that the Physics test that June was, according to the instructor, one of the hardest he had ever seen. I squeaked by with a "circled" 65, which meant it could later, upon review, be lowered to an "F." In addition I got circled 65's in both French and American History and was advised to go to Summer school in order to assure passing grades. This was my first experience in a public school and I had excellent instructors. I am sure that the school system provided their best teachers for these classes. I particularly remember the History instructor, a Mr. Fabiano, who was especially adept with the subject matter. In the final event, the exam had an essay question about F.D.R., who, it so happened, was a hero of mine, having read many books about him. I ended up scoring in the 90's. Thus ended my high school life as I prepared to start college. I would, however, stay at St. Andrew's as the first two years of college were part of the curriculum. There was no formal graduation ceremony from high school and there would be no class reunions. I remember only a few classmates from what I believe was a class of about 17. My Summer work plans were, of course, disrupted when I had to attend Summer School. Having turned

18 that June I was fully eligible to work but now that would have to wait another year.

The Fall of '57 brought new classmates as some were added who had gone to other high schools either in the city or from out of town. It was not required to go to the seminary immediately upon entering high school as I did. Those from out of town had to board whereas I continued to commute and there was a definite division between commuters and boarders and neither mingled with the other. As to commuting, I was fortunate to join a car pool with other seminarians and did not have to continue with the multiple bus transfers. This was a welcome relief during my last two years. New teachers also came along such as Father Cavanaugh, my English teacher, and Father Murphy, who taught Greek. One of my teachers was from high school, a Father Kenny. He taught me American history in my senior year and now taught Latin, in which we studied Livy and Ovid. I seemed to have gotten my equilibrium back and had no further difficulties with passing grades. Before I knew it I had advanced to the final year at St. Andrew's and graduated in June of 1959 in a full-blown ceremony. The Summer before I had worked at the city Police Department as a PBX operator, a job obtained through political patronage, and would return to it again in '59 before entering the major seminary. This was a job restricted only to men and I encountered people quite different than what I was used to. Suffice it to say that they broadened my horizons. Some of them referred to me as "padre," once they learned where I was going to school. The work was a bit stressful but I quickly adapted and got into the groove, working until about a week before I had to return to school.

What loomed ahead for me was the major seminary, St. Bernard's, and my last two years of college. I approached it with some trepidation as it would be the first time I had to live away from home, although I was still in the city. I would be going alone as my twin brother still had one more year at St. Andrew's before graduation. I was now halfway through the twelve year journey to the priesthood, but still not the master of my own destiny.

PART THREE

Advanced Training

CHAPTER 5

Major Seminary - Years of Commitment

And so, with not a little anticipation and trepidation, I went off to St. Bernard's Seminary early in the month of September, 1959, shortly after Labor Day. After checking in around 8 o'clock the night before and being assigned my room, I was awakened at 5:30 A.M. the following morning to begin a routine which would become second nature over the following three years.

St. Bernard's was founded in 1893 under Bishop Bernard McQuaid, Rochester's first bishop and was, unquestionably, the "gemstone" of his bishopric. Incidentally St. Andrew's Seminary was founded in 1870, only two years after Bishop McQuaid's installation as bishop in the newly formed Rochester Diocese. St. Bernard's would, however, always be the "apple of his eye."

Days were long, beginning at 5:30 and ending roughly at 10:00 with what was referred to as the "grand silence," when no conversation was permitted until the following day.

The day began with Mass at 6:30, followed by breakfast in what was referred to as the "refectory." Classes would begin at 8 o'clock and go until noon, at which time the students would meet in the chapel for the recitation of the Angelus prayer, followed by lunch. There would then be free time until two o'clock when classes resumed until 5 o'clock. The student body reassembled in the chapel at 5:30 for spiritual reading followed by supper at 6 o'clock. Students were then free until 7 o'clock when they reassembled in the chapel for recitation of the rosary. They were then expected to go to their rooms for private study. The day finally ended with night prayers at 10 o'clock in the chapel. This regimen was altered on Tuesdays and Fridays when, in the afternoon, students were expected to go on "church walks" from 1 until 4 o'clock to a designated parish, within walking distance of the seminary. Exceptions could be made to this, such as visiting someone at the old age home of St. Anne's, which, at the time, just happened to be only a 10 minute walk from the school. Also, permission could be given to visit the main library downtown in order to work on a school paper. As might be expected, there were always those who broke the rules and stopped in bars along the way. However, should this be reported to the rector and the identity of the individuals be ascertained, this would result in immediate expulsion from the seminary. Friday nights there was confession after dinner. Priests were brought in from outside the seminary for this weekly exercise. On Saturday there were half-day classes with the afternoons reserved for private study. After prayers in the chapel at 5 o'clock there was dinner and then, after a short recreation period, there was choir practice in the chapel at 7 o'clock, followed by private study until 10 o'clock prayers in the chapel. On Sunday there was breakfast followed by free time and then a High Mass in the chapel at 9 o'clock. Afterward there was free time until lunch and then recreation time until solemn benediction in the chapel at 5 o'clock, followed by dinner and then study time until 10 o'clock in the evening.

During my years at St. Bernard's, from 1959-1962, the rector was a Msgr. Craugh and you definitely knew who was in charge. One of the most intimidating individuals I have ever known, he would make the rectors at St Andrew's, to whom I have referred previously, seem warm and fuzzy by comparison. He definitely intended to put the fear, if not of God, then certainly of him, into you and I would have to say that he succeeded admirably. He could expel you from the school with a snap of his finger and there was no recourse to a higher authority. He had spent all of his priestly life at the seminary, being first the vice rector and then, in 1948, upon the retirement of his predecessor, succeeding to the rectorship. Having lost two fingers in an occupational accident when he was young, he was seemingly thus disqualified to become a priest, according to the old rules of Leviticus. However, exceptions can always be made and it was allowed that he be permitted to continue to ordination with the understanding that he would not take an assignment in a parish or any other position outside the confines of the seminary, but would remain there throughout his priesthood. He was only the fifth rector in the history of St. Bernard's. My most extended association with him was in an Italian language class I took as an elective one time a week.

My most memorable professors were Father Stanislaus Krolak, who taught Philosophy 101, Father Joseph Hogan, who taught Theology,

Father Robert McNamara, who taught Church History, and Father Joseph Brennan, who taught Sacred Scripture and who, incidentally, was the rector's nephew. There were actually two Father McNamaras, but I wasn't particularly enthralled by the other, Elmer, the name of whose course I don't even recall. Two of these professors, Fathers Hogan and Robert McNamara, achieved distinction above and beyond the confines of the seminary. Father Hogan would later become the seventh bishop of Rochester and Father McNamara was the official diocesan historian, having written a superb history of the Rochester Diocese.

My first year passed rather uneventfully and I looked forward to my twin brother joining me at the seminary in the Fall of 1960. I returned to my Summer job with the Rochester Police Department, being exposed again to life outside the cocoon of the seminary. This was my only real source of income and I looked forward to the bit of independence it gave me. Even though I was paid for eight hours work a day, I actually worked only four as I rotated with another operator, with each of us being on one hour and then off an hour. It was shift work and I could work either days, 8-4, evenings, 4-12, or midnight, 12-8. Being somewhat of a night person, I actually preferred the midnight shift, which was, incidentally, the least busy. I got in, I would guesstimate, about 12 weeks of work.

School began again soon enough with the significant difference that my twin was now also in attendance, although a year behind me. One added benefit was that I could always be assured of a walking partner when Tuesday and Friday afternoon came around. Of course, we did not always join up on these but did so frequently. I remember that on occasions that we did so, we would often pass one of the priests from the seminary who was returning from his walk somewhere and he would always remark as he went by "There they are together." I always thought he was a bit odd and had minimal contact with him in my classes. He was an English teacher and not particularly impressive I might add.

My second year was more challenging as I had a course in Metaphysical Philosophy taught by Father Hart, who liked to use Latin as much as possible. The material itself was demanding enough without this extra factor. I struggled through the class and hoped he wouldn't call on me, which, of course, he sometimes did. I think he thought he was smarter than he actually was and tried to impress people with his seeming brilliance. At this stage in my life I could, like many others, be easily intimidated. It would be only later that I would realize he wasn't all that brilliant after all.

This was the year of the Kennedy-Nixon election and, of course, we were allowed to go to vote and had to go to our home polling place, which was just a few yards from our house. Since elections are on Tuesday anyway this was a convenient substitute for the afternoon church walk. This was a big event being our first time voting and we were pulling for Kennedy. No newspapers or radios were allowed at school but, of course, someone always broke the rule and I knew by that night that Kennedy was the likely winner.

In June of 1961 I had finished college but there was no ceremony or presenting of diplomas. I still had four more years of study if I were to be ordained and I thus passed seamlessly to the study of Theology. The school was divided into Philosophy Hall and Theology Hall, and I was now taking classes in the latter. Now that I had seemingly gotten through college, I began to question more and more what reason did I have to continue on my present course if I didn't really want to be ordained. However, I decided to go the extra mile and not make any hasty decision. I was confronted with the dilemma that, even if I didn't want to be a priest, I didn't really know what else I was searching for. Anyway, I worked my regular Summer job again and then returned to the seminary to begin what was technically graduate school, although no extra degree would be awarded. The seminary did not have the authority to confer anything higher than a baccalaureate.

More and more I was coming to the conclusion that while I was involved in priesthood study I was not really committed. It's like the old joke abut ham and eggs – the chicken is involved but the pig is committed. In order to satisfy myself I talked to the spiritual director who really didn't resolve my quandary. However, I was probably just looking for someone to confirm a decision that I had, for all practical purposes, already made for myself. Having resolved not to return at the end of the '62 school year, I notified the rector of my decision and then went to get my academic transcript only to be told that I had not been granted a degree as my score in my major, though passing, wasn't considered high enough to grant me a B.A. This all seemed a bit strange as I thought I should have been told this at the end of the previous academic year. I had always assumed a priest had to have a college degree but, apparently, that wasn't true in my case.

With this untoward turn of events, my future was already decided. I would have to get a college degree from some other school. I applied to St. John Fisher College, which was in Rochester and to Niagara University up in Niagara, N.Y. near Buffalo. Both were run by Catholic religious orders. I was accepted by each but there were drawbacks in both instances. I could complete the necessary course work for a degree in one academic year, but St. John Fisher had a rule that it would not confer a degree on anyone who spent less than two years there. Niagara would let me complete my coursework in one year but I would have to board there. Between the tuition and boarding at Niagara and the extra year at St. John Fisher, while living at home, the expense would probably be about equal so I finally, after living three years away from home, opted to live at home and do the extra year. I still had my Summer job and could also work part-time during the school year, which I eventually did. I got a job around the holidays working as a sales clerk at a haberdashery downtown. When that was over I landed a job at the local newspaper office working the switchboard at night, two nights a week, Saturday and Sunday. Mondays were really difficult as I had to go directly from the job to school, which made for a very long day. However I am getting a bit ahead of myself.

Here I was, after nine years of living a seminary life, ready to face the challenge of living outside the bubble and deciding what to do with the rest of my life. Since Philosophy was my major course of study in the seminary I opted to pursue it as my major while pursuing my quest for a B.A. St. John Fisher, being an all male college, my environment would not be significantly different than what I had experienced over the previous 19 years of my life. A new chapter was about to begin.

CHAPTER 6

Still in the Shadows

I returned to my usual Summer employ before entering St. John Fisher but not without having to jump through some hoops. The city had gone from Republican to Democrat the previous November and, as I was registered Republican, I was told I would have to re-register as a Democrat in order to retain my Summer employ. I agreed to do this and went back to work with the Police Department yet felt in my bones that this would be my final gig and, as it turned out, I was right. The Summer passed quickly and I preferred not to let it be known that I was no longer in the seminary as I honestly felt it was really not any of my co-workers business. Also, I wanted to avoid the questions that would inevitably follow.

I entered the Junior class at Fisher just after Labor Day, with not a little apprehension and trepidation. Oddly enough, the feast day of St. John Fisher is June 22, the same day as my birthday. Whether this was providential or merely coincidental is impossible to determine. What most immediately struck me was the informality of the Basilian Fathers as opposed to the strict formality I had encountered with the secular clergy. This was a most refreshing change. I had to meet with my faculty advisor, Father Miller, who was chairman of the Philosophy department, to arrange my schedule for the coming year. I would have to take courses in two of my bête-noires, Science and Math, as they were required for graduation. I struggled through, however, and found it easier going after that. In order to help support myself, I took a part-time job as a telemarketer with Life magazine. Selling not being my strong suit, I failed to garner many new subscriptions and was politely told, after about a month, that my services were no longer needed. After about another month I got a part-time job as a sales clerk with a local clothing store that was hiring for the upcoming holiday season. This was more to my liking as people had to come to me rather than I having to go to them. This lasted until January when inventory had been completed. I was not to remain unemployed for long as I secured a job as a telephone operator with the local Gannett newspaper. This was weekends only, including Saturday from 11 P.M. until 7 A.M. and a double shift on Sunday from 3 P.M. until 7 A.M. on Monday. The company preferred to have a man on duty at those times as the area was not considered particularly safe after hours on weekends. This was a little difficult for me on Monday as I had to go directly from work to school but I persevered and kept this job until I graduated from college.

My social life was fairly circumscribed and I felt that I had not yet fully emerged from the shadows of my seminary past, which constituted almost a decade of my life. I fell into a routine of going to the movies on Saturday night with my older brother, who was a school teacher and still living at home. Then I was much occupied with my school work and outside employment and, as a good upstanding Catholic, was still living a chaste life. Impinging me further was my lack of a car, although I had obtained a driver's license in the Summer of '62. Nor did I have money for its proper upkeep even if I somehow obtained one. Besides not having money for socializing I found it necessary to secure a $500 loan from a local bank in order to finance my final year of college as my family could offer no help. To say I was living close to the cushion would be an accurate description of my situation.

At the end of my Junior year, I was advised that I wouldn't be hired again by the city and, in light of the politics involved, this came as not particularly surprising. Since the county remained in Republican hands I sought employment there and was told that, should a re-register again as a Republican, I could obtain Summer work there. I agreed to again play this game of musical chairs and was hired by the Sheriff's Office as a radio dispatcher. This job required more responsibility and was more stressful than my previous one as I had to not only answer calls from the public but also had to dispatch cars and/or ambulances to various locations as circumstances required. A fringe benefit was that I could have lunch in the kitchen of the office and oftentimes ate in the company of the sheriff himself. That Summer was particularly momentous as there was a double homicide of two teenagers out in Pittsford, a suburb of Rochester, and heightened activity around the office. In the event, the double murder was not solved and to this day, fifty years later, remains a cold case. There were rumors that the detectives had a person of interest but didn't have enough evidence to make an arrest.

Of course the most memorable event that occurred during my Senior year was the assassination of President Kennedy on Friday, November 22. School was dismissed early and the following Monday was declared a National Holiday. It had been 62 years since a president was assassinated and thus an event which many people would not experience in their lifetimes. To say it was traumatic would be a gross understatement.

As I entered my final year at Fisher, I had the option of taking many electives and so, of course, loaded up on courses that I liked and that were my strong points. I thus earned a high enough GPA to make the Dean's List in the Spring of '64. It was at this time that I had to seriously consider my future upon graduating. Father Miller was willing to recommend me for graduate work in Philosophy but, after 19 years of uninterrupted schooling, I opted instead to apply for federal civil service employment and took the FSEE (Federal Service Entrance Exam) in January. I scored a respectable high-80's mark and could be assured that job offerings would materialize by the time I graduated. Graduation came around quickly on June 7 and, shortly thereafter, I received an offer from the Social Security Administration for a job as a Benefit Examiner at one of their processing centers in New York City. I flew down with my first cousin and was interviewed for the job and then spent one overnight in the city before returning to Rochester. It wasn't long after that I received notice that I had been hired and would begin training on Monday, July 6. Being out of work I eagerly anticipated getting started on my new career. However, I was soon thereafter notified that the training would not begin until two weeks later on July 20. Not having much to do at home I filled much of my time reading or visiting a cousin of mine who lived across the city.

Soon enough it was time to depart and, not knowing anyone in New York, I opted to stay at a YMCA on West 23rd street. However, I didn't find this particularly to my liking and, after asking around, found out that there was a men's Catholic boarding house called Kolping House, on East 88th, a better part of the city, so I moved over there.

About half way through my training I was contacted by the Selective Service and advised that I would have to take a physical exam for possible induction into the Army.

After much serious thought, I concluded that if I had to give two years of my life in service to my country it would be better spent in the Peace Corps, a then very popular government program. This was not an effort to be a draft dodger as it was made clear that service in the Peace Corps did not, in and of itself, disqualify me from later induction into the service. I went ahead and applied and, to my surprise, was accepted fairly quickly. Not being particularly enamored of my civil service job anyway, I had no hesitation about accepting this offer. I notified the office of my decision to terminate and, immediately after Election Day, returned to Rochester to get ready for my new adventure. It was during this time that I last saw my father who wanted to take me out to dinner. He disagreed with my decision to join the Corps but didn't belabor the point. He also asked for forgiveness for neglecting me as a parent. I very sanctimoniously replied that such forgiveness had to come from God. I am sure that as a more mature and less narrow-minded individual, I would not have given such an answer, but such was the legacy of my overly conservative Catholic upbringing.. My father died only 18 days later, after I was already in Hawaii for training. I don't remember him ever telling me that he loved me and that is probably because, in reality, he really didn't.

My training for the Peace Corps was to be done in Hilo, Hawaii. I had to undergo intensive language training in Gujarati as I was being trained in agricultural work for a project in Gujarat, India. I didn't reflect upon it at the time but, in retrospect, this was certainly a mismatch for someone with a Liberal Arts background and from an urban environment. However, naively believing that father, in this instance, the federal government, knows best, I concurred. As part of the training, psychiatrists were constantly hovering about, observing your behavior and everyone was obliged to have an interview with one of them. Unbeknownst to me at the time there was a "selection out" process by which trainees could be released from the program if deemed unfit for one reason or another. As it turned out, I and a handful of others were selected out by mid-December and given tickets to return home. While not formally stated it was implied that I might have entered the Corps simply to avoid the draft or that I, due to my extensive religious background and rigid views, might attempt to proselitize the Indians. Neither of these conclusions was valid but the decision about me was not appealable and so I arrived back in Rochester a few days before Christmas.

The next months were difficult as I was unemployed and a weak candidate for employment due to my draft status. I reapplied for a Federal position but that doesn't happen overnight. I was, however, contacted by HEW about a job as an agent tracking down the sources of venereal disease among carriers in New York City. This wasn't particularly appealing but I didn't reject it outright. In the meantime, I was sent up to Buffalo twice for physical exams pursuant to induction into the Army. With no decision being forthcoming from the Army, I was still in limbo so decided to accelerate the process by contacting my senator, who at the time was Robert Kennedy, in order to resolve this situation. To my surprise I was quickly contacted by the local draft board, somewhat importuned that

I had contacted Kennedy, and was quickly sent back to Buffalo. It was determined that my vision was problematical and the examining doctor left it up to me as to whether I would accept induction, For reasons that at the time weren't entirely clear I consented but believe that subliminally I wanted to refute those who thought I was a draft dodger. Also, with my civilian future somewhat murky and having had one previous option rejected this was an opportunity to regain some stability and take charge of my life. Apparently I had become something of a minor celebrity as the commanding officer of the installation singled me out and congratulated me on my upcoming military service. Robert Kennedy opened the door but now I had to walk through. Little did I realize it at the time but the next two years would be a true watershed in my life, setting me on a job course that would continue with but a brief interruption for the next thirty years of my life.

PART FOUR

Outside the Cocoon

CHAPTER 7

You're in the Army Now

Thus began my two-year Army career as I was hustled off by train from Buffalo to Fort Dix, New Jersey with nothing but the clothes on my back. Upon arrival there, I would be issued Army apparel and my civilian clothes would be sent back to my home address. The Army would also take my picture to send back home to assure everyone, I presume, that I was actually in the Army and was alive and well.

Given that basic training was only eight weeks long and the Vietnam War was heating up, the days were filled with activity and not a second was wasted. Days began at 0530 and went with lights out at 2200. My platoon sergeant, an Irishman whose name I do not recall, was neither the harshest nor the most lenient among those in command of the four platoons in the company. He mentioned once that "his balls were aching to go fight the Viet Cong in Vietnam." One island of refuge from the daily grind of training was going to the Catholic chapel on the base. I had to request permission to go but this would not be denied for fear that I would claim religious discrimination. One thing that struck me was the superior quality of the sermons, or as they now call them, homilies, which were delivered. Possibly this was because the cream of the crop among the clergy chose to serve as chaplains in the military. Who can say? It wasn't until much later that another soldier in my platoon told me that he was motivated to go back to church because he was impressed by my regular attendance at Sunday services. Perhaps it's more than a shibboleth that actions do speak louder than words after all. I have maintained contact with this individual over the years even though we are separated by many miles.

The weeks sped by rather quickly, what with the intensive schedule, and, before I knew it, I was on the cusp of being assigned to AIT (Advanced Individual Training). Since I was not an enlistee, but merely a draftee, my fate hung solely on the whims of the military bureaucracy. I had no choice in what my onward assignment would be although a battery of tests I took early in my training would help the powers that be determine what MOS (Military Occupational Specialty) I would be delegated to. As fate would have it I was given orders to report to the Signal Corps school at Fort Gordon, Georgia after a brief period of leave between basic training and this new assignment. I returned home to New York for what would turn out to be my last time spent in the home I had grown up and lived in, almost uninterruptedly, for the past 24 years. My grandmother had died the previous month and my mother was in the process of selling the property, pursuant to getting remarried later that Summer.

Going to Georgia would be my first experience living in the South and I looked forward to it with high anticipation but not without a little foreboding as to what my new assignment would bring. I was pleasantly surprised to learn that the environment in advanced training was much less stressful than what I had only recently experienced. The training at the U.S. Army Southeastern Signal Corps School (USASESCS) would last for approximately 8 weeks. Being much attuned to classroom instruction I quickly adjusted to my new challenge. Nearing the end of my AIT (Advanced Individual Training) I was informed that the Signal Corps School was going to initiate a pilot program of using new trainees as instructors in the facility so as to free up grizzled veterans who wanted to volunteer for duty in Vietnam. Furthermore, I was one of those chosen to be a part of this new program. This opportunity seemed too good to be true and I quickly complied, knowing moreover that, in the Army, going with the flow is much to be preferred to swimming against the tide. One of the best lessons I learned from my military service was that if the powers that be couldn't make you do something, they could most certainly make you wish that you had. With this serendipitous turn of events, my remaining tour at Fort Gordon was defined and I was given the designation of "permanent party," meaning I had special privileges such as being able to go to the front of the chow line, not having to stand inspections, and not having to sign out and then back in for my leave pass when going off base. The gods had definitely shined on me and I wasn't about to look a gift horse in the face.

Being a regular attendant at the base Catholic chapel I drew the attention of the Catholic chaplain, a Major Robert Beckers, who asked me to be an assistant to him even though he had an enlisted man officially assigned to him. I soon learned that theirs was not a particularly commodious relationship, thus the need for a semi-replacement, as it were. Major Beckers was a curious individual, being a licensed airplane pilot and, it was rumored, better able to fly an airplane than to drive a car. I had one experience riding with him in his private plane and his skills were quite adequate. On Sundays after Mass, I would catechize a group of trainees for about an hour and then the major, his official assistant, another assistant priest and I would go out to his apartment in the suburbs of Augusta, have breakfast, watch some tv, and, on occasion, go to a movie later at one of the base theaters. I very much looked forward to these weekly outings as it got me away from the confines of the barracks for a few hours.

Back at the Signal Corps school, I settled into the routine of teaching the new recruits in the mechanics of how a communications center operates and what they could expect when they actually got assigned to one. There were also regular Army sergeants working along with us, with there being a mix, as I recall, of six draftees like myself, known as "U.S.s" and four enlisted sergeants, known as "RAs". Presentations were rotated among us and there were generous coffee breaks and a leisurely lunch hour. Occasionally on Friday afternoons, I would take some leave time and play golf with one of my fellow draftees and one of the sergeant instructors at a nine-hole course on the base. It was mainly for the exercise as, to put it mildly, my golf skills left a lot to be desired. After short formations on Saturday morning, everyone was dismissed until the cycle began again Monday morning. I was free to go into Augusta, hang around the base, or just spend time reading or watching tv in the barracks.

In the Summer of 1966 I was contacted by a military member of the K. of C., asking if I wanted to join. Apparently there was a massive recruitment campaign in progress and I could be inducted in one day, receiving all of the first three degrees in one fell swoop. The Knights of Columbus is the largest Catholic fraternity and the third largest fraternity in the world. More out of curiosity than anything else I consented and, on a Sunday afternoon, was driven down to Atlanta for the initiation, which lasted until early evening. It was one of the most traumatic experiences of my life and I was sworn to secrecy as to what transpires, the reason for which, of course, became self-evident to me once I learned the purpose of the initiation. It was only later that I would discover that the fraternity's ideals were observed more as an exception than as a rule, but then this could probably be affirmed of any human organization, so what was I to expect? However, still being unwise as to the ways of the world, in short naïve, I saw it only through rose-colored glasses. It was the only fraternity that I ever had or, for that matter, ever would join.

It was shortly after this that, during one of the coffee breaks at the training center, one of the staff sergeants mentioned that he wanted to join the Foreign Service of the State Department but, due to the fact that he was married, he was considered ineligible. At that time the Department was hiring only single people interested in working overseas. He thought I might be interested as I was single and had the background in communications center operations that they were looking for. Having never lived overseas and having had a rather sheltered background, this all seemed very exciting. Also I had to start pondering my future once I left the Army and here was what seemed like a golden opportunity. I sent in the required application and before I knew it the Department responded with an offer to bring me up to Washington, all expenses paid, for the requisite physiological and psychological testing. At the time - remember this was in the '60's-anyone determined to be homosexual would be immediately disqualified. I spent two days undergoing the various exams and then returned to Fort Gordon. Not long after, an investigator visited the base and inquired of my superiors as to my character, work ethic, etc. This was a positive sign that I was still being considered for the position but, as a default, I also took the Federal Service Entrance Exam again, almost guaranteeing that I would get a federal government position one way or the other. Hopefully, I would hear something positive by the time I was discharged, which was now less than six months away.

The rest of my tour continued apace, and hardly before I knew it I was getting my discharge and returning to civilian life. The day after I returned to Rochester, where I stayed with my mother, I received notification that I had indeed been hired by State and would be notified shortly as to my onward assignment. It was only shortly after that I received a phone call advising me that my assignment was to Bern, Switzerland and that my training would begin July 7. This was now May so I didn't have all that long to wait, but was, nonetheless, antsy to get started. It just so happened that there was at the time an Expo '67 up in Montreal, Canada so, to get a change of venue, I went up there for a few days. My social life back in Rochester was, per usual, nothing noteworthy. However, a cousin of mine, who lived across the city and whom I visited occasionally, introduced me to her roomer, a single girl about my age. We dated and she even invited me to visit her parents and stay overnight at their home. Since it was no secret that I was going overseas, nothing developed beyond a "boy meets girl" relationship.

I entered on my new adventure over the weekend of Labor Day 1967 when I departed Kennedy airport on my way to Bern, Switzerland. It was somewhat ironic that I joined the Army, presumably to see the world, but never left the U.S. and here I was going overseas with the State Department. I had finally escaped the protective cocoon of Catholicism as well as that of an all-male environment.

CHAPTER 8

The Foreign Service:
A World Beyond Home

On Labor Day weekend of 1967 I left JFK airport for Geneva, Switzerland and thence to Berne, the Swiss capital. I was met there by my supervisor and taken to my temporary living quarters at the Silvahof Hotel, right next to the American Embassy. That night Tom and his wife, Elaine, would host a welcoming dinner for me at their home where I also met their two daughters, Sandra and Kim. The next morning I was driven to the Catholic Church by Tom and witnessed my first Mass in a foreign country. I suspect that many of the congregants were expats as this particular area of Switzerland was predominantly Protestant. Here again the Catholic Church served as a continuous link during watershed events in my life.

I quickly adapted to the comcenter routine in the American Embassy. This was my first real experience with the actual inner workings of cable preparation and the transmission and reception of telegrams but I found that my past military school training and teaching environment in a simulated comcenter at Fort Gordon served me well. The environment in the church of State was rather stilted however. My co-workers referred to each other as "Thomas" and "Catherine' instead of the more user-friendly "Tom" and "Cathy." I found this a bit off-putting. Oddly enough I was addressed by my nickname as maybe "Richard" was even too formal for them.

Housing was tight in the city and, in addition, I required a furnished apartment. As a result I was consigned to the Silvahof Hotel for three months but, just as my allowance for temporary housing was due to expire, I landed an apartment just a block from the embassy. This was truly fortuitous as my job would sometimes require me to answer what were referred to as NIACT (Night Action) telegrams after hours. Luckily I was rarely woken up in the middle of the night.

I had barely settled in when the Christmas holidays rolled around and this was my first away from home and a somewhat lonely one at that. I can't say I was sorry to see the New Year holiday come quickly and then the ensuing re-entrance into the old routine. 1968, an eventful year in and of itself, was to become a particularly eventful one for me. In March, while "on duty," part of my responsibility was to meet the diplomatic courier and take him to the embassy where he would deliver his pouches. It so happened that, on this occasion, that transaction was to transpire on a Saturday. It also just so happened that I was invited to a cocktail party that evening and, inadvertently, had failed to refill my gas tank before going to the event. When I had to leave for the embassy I only then realized that my tank was almost empty and I would not be able to make it in time to meet the courier. This necessitated calling my supervisor and telling him my situation which resulted in his having to do the job that night. Suffice it to say he was not at all pleased and the following week he told me in a private conference that he was going to recommend that I be sent back to D.C. Lest this seem to be more of an overreaction than warranted, although an overreaction it certainly was, I had the previous December informed him that I planned on taking the Foreign Service Officer Exam in order to improve my job status. He, of course, took a dim view of this as it would then necessitate my having to be replaced before my two-year tour was up, assuming, of course, that I passed the test and was offered an assignment as a Foreign Service Officer, all very speculative to say the least. Further, I had mentioned offhand to another employee at a cocktail party that I felt maybe my present position wasn't really my "cup of tea," as the saying goes. I was also a little under the weather at the time. It seemed my Foreign Service career would die aborning but the Admin Officer, assessing the situation for its true worth, judged that this was not worthy of further action and that I should stay at post. As might be expected the environment in the comcenter remained a bit chilly until my supervisor went on home leave the following June. It was also during June that my first family visitors arrived, my second cousins with whom I was quite close. Besides seeing Switzerland I took them to London and Dublin. These few weeks together were a memorable time for us all.

A truly high point of '68, however, was my Eastertime visit to Rome. Although I had never been there before I somehow intuitively found my way from my lodging in downtown Rome to the Vatican. It happened to be Holy Thursday and the Pope, Paul VI, was just leaving St. Peter's Square, standing in his Mercedes. I was close enough to get a good photo and, as he stared at me, I had the distinct impression he did not approve. Over the following week I was to visit highlights of the Vatican such as the crypt below the main altar, the burial place of former popes, and to see the Sistine Chapel, a truly unforgettable experience. I was later again to visit the Vatican over Easter of '70, but this first impression was the most impressionable, if you will.

My work life was to take a dramatic turn in the Summer of '68. The supervisor was on leave back in the U.S. and my co-worker was hospitalized with back problems. As luck would or wouldn't have it, an international crisis erupted in Czechoslovakia that June. Doing the workload of three people would have been challenging enough but I now had the extra burden of handling an increased amount of cable traffic due to this turn of events. It was necessary that I work an inordinate amount of time for which I could not be paid overtime but, rather, what was referred to as compensatory time which would be accrued and then be available for use as leave time at some future point. I believe I accumulated about 68 hours as a result of the extra workload and, not surprisingly, never had the opportunity to exercise it. With the return of the co-worker after about a two week interval and, later, the return of my supervisor, the work environment mercifully reverted to its normal pace.

That Fall I had the pleasure of having my twin brother pay a visit for about ten days. Besides visiting high points in country we also went off for a few days to Germany. This was the first time I had seen him since joining the Foreign Service. It was also that Autumn that I decided I would spend the Christmas holiday back home and made reservations to fly back on a non-commercial flight and stay in the U.S. for about two weeks. This arrangement was made through a U.S.-Swiss Association, formed to foster closer relations between the U.S. and Switzerland. The accommodations were bare bones but, at a rock-bottom price, it was worth it. It was over this vacation period that two significant events occurred, neither of which turned out to be serendipitous. My stepfather was in the hospital and in the final stages of succumbing to cancer. We both knew it was the last time we would see each other. On what seemed a lighter note at the time, I was introduced to the daughter of a good friend of my mother, who, upon learning I was living in Switzerland, expressed an interest in visiting me there, although, in the event, that would not happen for another year. As 1969 rolled around I expected that I would be looking at a new assignment come the following September. However, my supervisor asked me in May if I would be amenable to extending my current tour four months until January of 1970. At the time that was the longest extension permissible. Finding Switzerland very agreeable I readily consented. It seemed that the onetime "goat" had turned into a "hero."

In July I enjoyed a most pleasant interlude when my mother and older brother visited me for about a week. We hit some high spots such as the Jungfrau and Lucerne, which was home to one of the best restaurants in Switzerland, the name of which escapes me. Time passed quickly and I was sorry to see them go when the time came. I thought that would be my last visitation from family but my mother returned for another stay of about 10 days later in the Fall. My older brother was back at work teaching school and my mother was presently alone, my stepfather having died the previous January, so this was a good opportunity for her.

My life proceeded apace and I found out in the Fall that the woman I had met the past December was planning a trip to visit me the following December. Learning this, my current feminine co-worker, who would be on leave in the U.S. over the holidays, offered, without my asking, to let this visitor use her apartment, which was just up the street from me. Forbid the thought that I would co-habit with the opposite sex. To say that the State Department has a puritanical frame of mind would be a gross understatement. Suffice it to say that my visitor stayed one night in the co-worker's apartment. This woman, once married and divorced, was a raving women's libber. This hardly endeared her to me and the end of her two-week visit couldn't come soon enough to suit me. For me the only memorable part of the visit was a short trip taken to Paris over New Year's, a highlight being dining at La Tous D'Argent, one of the most famous restaurants in the world. Early in January my live-in visitor returned to the U.S. and I was not to see or hear from her again until I myself returned stateside at the end of my tour in Switzerland.

It was also during the previous December that I was given a Meritorious Honor Award based on my one-man stand in the Summer of '68, 18 months previously. Things do not happen quickly at State.

As to my tour it seemed to be never-ending. I was requested again to take an extension of four more months, bringing me to May, 1970 and before that would terminate, I was asked to take another final four additional months. By law that was as much as could be allowed and so my original two-year tour turned into one of three years and I have to say that I thoroughly enjoyed every one of them. Initially my onward assignment was to be Frankfurt, Germany, but that was rescinded and I was given Saigon, South Vietnam. This was not surprising since the Department feels the need to balance plush assignments with hardship ones so that its employees carry an equitable share of the load. At the time little did I realize that this next deployment would be a most pivotal one not only professionally but, even more importantly, personally, but more about that later. So far I had not been successful in entering the Officer Corps of the Foreign Service but had also decided not to peremptorily cut short my supposed career with State. Still I knew in my bones that, unless I pursued a vocation more in alignment with my educational background, I would never be truly satisfied in my present occupation.

It was during my subsequent home leave that I was to experience a sort of déjà-vu experience reminiscent of that I had before my assignment to Switzerland, but this was to have monumental repurcussions. The threads of this life-changing event will be woven as I continue my narrative in the next chapter. Come what may my three years in Switzerland were and remain some of the most memorable of my life.

CHAPTER 9

A New Assignment and a Termination

My home leave in Rochester before going onward with my new assignment was somewhat unsettling. I knew more about what I didn't want to do than, conversely, what I did want. The Foreign Service had opened up a whole new world to me and I wasn't about to slam the door shut without a clearer discernment of what I intended to do going forward. After my unfortunate encounter with the live-in visitor mentioned previously I was skeptical and wary of such a reoccurrence, feeling somewhat vulnerable in the process. My mother, perhaps subconsciously sensing that feminine friendship might be a good elixir at this time, let it be known to a neighbor that I was home and, being advised that this neighbor's niece was also seemingly at loose ends, arranged to have us meet. A rendez-vous was arranged at a time just thirteen days before I was to go back overseas. On the face of it this might have seemed foolhardy since what would be the purpose of getting acquainted with someone over such a short space of time if, in fact, there was any interest in getting acquainted at all? In the event the get-together was confirmed by me and the niece, more out of a sense of duty to those who initiated it rather than out of any hope that it would be of any real significance. Neither of the principles involved could have been more wrong. There was an instant physical attraction at the outset and, as later events would make painfully clear, an overwillingess to see something that wasn't really there, fueled by vulnerabilities both of us had from recent bad relationships. We went out almost daily over the remaining days before my leaving for Vietnam. The night before I was to leave we went to a movie and then to her house so I could meet her parents. I felt as though I were on the "hot seat" as I had the distinct impression I was being eyed suspiciously.

My new-found friend apparently had apprehensions about how I would be received and, I would attest, justifiably so. Her parents were polite but a bit cool. After about an hour's time, I was driven home and, before I could get out of the car, was smothered by kisses. This totally unexpected event had a profound effect as I had never had a woman react to me quite that way. Suffice it to say, I left the next morning with a heavy heart and mixed emotions. Little did I know that my emotions were to become much more mixed and confusing over the next few months.

I had a brief stopover with my mother at my twin brother's home in Salt Lake City and then another short interlude in San Francisco, from which my mother returned to New York. I arrived in Saigon on November 20 and was taken to my temporary living quarters at a downtown hotel. It was about a month before I was relocated to my permanent residence in a USAID building on a road leading directly to the embassy, which was only about a 10 minute walk away. I became quickly caught up in my new work environment, helping to staff a 24/7 operation. In the meantime I kept up a steady correspondence with the woman I had left behind in New York in what amounted to what was essentially a "pen-pal" relationship. The holidays went by rather uneventfully and soon thereafter my routine took on a rather predictable pattern of work and then often going to the American Embassy Club for dinner and, on occasion, a movie afterwards at the same location. However, within a few months my life was to be changed dramatically in ways that I could not then even imagine.

Even though it was frowned upon by the State Department, associations, even liaisons, if you will, with foreign nationals were almost inevitable, considering one was living and working in their country. After a little over five months, I began a relationship with a Vietnamese woman, who, though eight and a half years younger, was an oasis in what was then for me a desert of separation from someone I had left in the U.S. and had known for less than two weeks. Our relationship was essentially that of "pen pals," although I didn't objectivize it that way then. However, my new-found Vietnamese friend had the distinct advantage of physical proximity whereas my friend in the States was more than 8,000 miles away. This had the inevitable consequence of my forging a stronger emotional bond with this "forbidden" foreign national. A month before this all began, I had, in a fit of homesickness and loneliness, proposed by letter to my friend in New York, a proposal to which, amazingly, she responded in the affirmative. Meanwhile, back in Saigon, I continued my relationship with the Vietnamese national. From there the "actio in distans" courtship of my New York lover took on a life of it's own and, if the truth be told, rapidly spun out of control, whether or not either of us realized it at the time and apparently we didn't or just didn't want to. It was agreed that we would get formally engaged in July, 1971 via an R&R which I would take to Hawaii, having her meet me there from New York. All this proceeded apace while I was becoming continuously involved with what was an enduring relationship with my Vietnamese friend, who, incidentally, wanted me to meet her mother. This should have set off alarm bells and raised red flags, but it didn't. Is it possible to love two people simultaneously? I submit that it is but, eventually, one will take priority over the other. I made no secret of the fact I was getting engaged but this did not seem to affect our relationship. After the Hawaii vacation, during which my mother was also present, and engagement, I resumed by previous liaison with my Vietnamese friend, naively believing that somehow things would work themselves out. Not wishing to crush feelings, or, perhaps, not having the moral courage to resolve this one way or the other, I drifted along in a state of duplicity and disillusionment. There was another complicating factor in this triangle, of which I was implicitly aware although it was never explicitly stated at the time. My Vietnamese friend would never leave her father as he was her favorite, a bond made even stronger when his other daughter was killed during the Tet offensive of 1968.

Before I was even halfway through my second assignment with State, I had decided that the Foreign Service was not intellectually or vocationally satisfying. Resolved to continue my education as a means of a more satisfying career, I chose to pursue a graduate degree in Religious Education so as ultimately to qualify as a Religion Teacher. By chance I came upon an article by a Dr. Martin Lang, head of the Religion Department at Fairfield University in Fairfield, Connecticut. This thunderbolt from out of the blue gave me the resolve to apply for its graduate school in Religious Education. To my surprise, I not only got accepted but also was offered a half-tuition scholarship. This turn of events greatly pleased my fiancée in New York as it resolved any doubt as to whether I would deploy to another assignment with State or resign to pursue my education and, hopefully, a new career. She was overwhelmingly in favor of the latter as, of course, so was I. This was not something I discussed with my Vietnamese friend since she was already resigned to the fact that I intended to leave after my assignment and return to New York.

My tour in Saigon continued apace to its inexorable end with my emotions caught up in a vortex of mixed feelings and guilt pangs. Although I felt committed by this time to my fiancée in New York, I was at the same time increasingly attached to my Vietnamese friend. As my final days approached before returning to the States, I was increasingly aware that all this would end badly as, eventually, it did. Neither of us was able to sleep the night before my departure. She asked me if I wanted to end the relationship upon leaving Saigon and I said that I did not. There was a tearful departure the following morning and I boarded my flight in a depressed mood. I had put myself in this predicament and now saw it as a lose-lose situation. I had to spend three days in Washington in order to process out as I was resigning from State. All too soon I was arriving back in Rochester where I was met at the airport by my mother and my fiancée. Rationalizing that I was doing the right thing, although my feelings were mixed, I immersed myself in the plans for the wedding which was only a little more than five weeks away. I found that I was caught up in a whirlpool of emotions and unable or unwilling to extricate myself. There were veiled vibes from my prospective mother-in-law that alerted me to the doubts she was having about the wisdom of this marriage. Prescient though she was she also may have felt it difficult, if not impossible, to go against the fast-moving current of events. She said that she needed to get to know me better and, possibly, this implied that so too did her daughter. We made some small talk and I always came away with the impression, later to be eminently verified, that she had reservations about me and my impending marriage to my fiancée. There was little communication with her husband as his wife was undeniably the ruling force in the family and he knew better than to step out of his place, as it were.

The month of June passed quickly with a high point being a birthday celebration for me with some of my family members attending at my fiancee's house. Only nine days remained until our wedding on July 1. During that month I was also introduced to various members of her family, aunts, uncles, cousins, etc. The final event was a practice ceremony at the church the evening before the wedding with a dinner at my fiancee's house afterward.

The big day arrived with pleasant weather and a case of last-minute nerves with respect to my soon to be bride, although, I must admit, I felt a satisfying sense of composure as though I were merely accepting the inevitable, which, in truth, I was. The ceremony was given the full panoply that the Catholic rituals allowed, all of which was recorded by a movie camera. Outside the church afterword occurred what was what I thought to be a bizarre remark made to me by her father. He asserted very ominously that if I failed to take care of his daughter properly, or words to that effect, he would hunt me down like a tiger in order to get revenge. Not exactly the touchy-feely words one would expect to hear from one's brand new father-in-law. Then came the reception with the traditional festivities: the bride dancing with her father, the groom dancing with his mother-in-law, the tossing of the garter, etc. By late afternoon, my newly-minted bride and I were off to a local hotel where the climax – pun intended – was to take place. The next afternoon we returned to her parents home and got ready for our honeymoon trip to Puerto Rico. We would be leaving the following morning and staying for about a week. When the honeymoon ended, my wife was obviously happy to get back to the nest, as it were, upon returning home and said so in so many words. Was it the trip or, perhaps, I, that was boring?

There ensued about a six-week stay at her house, briefly interrupted by a short trip in mid-August to Fairfield so that we could check the lay of the land and, hopefully, secure living arrangements prior to relocating later that month. The Fall term would begin just after Labor Day. We found a one bedroom furnished apartment, which, in actuality, was the downstairs of a private residence and signed a one year lease. The one car garage was included. My wife was desirous of working full-time, which was, of course, agreeable to me, if that was her desire, although I didn't insist on it. She obtained a full-time teaching position at a private school, Milford Academy, in Milford, Connecticut, about a fifteen mile drive from Fairfield. For myself, I would be going to school full-time but also wanted at least a part-time, if not a full-time job. I reasoned that this was doable as I would be going to school in the early and late evening hours, unlike my schedule when I was in college. As it turned out, I quickly secured at job at the University working in the kitchen, offloading food supplies and storing them in the freezers. I had to work full-time Monday through Friday and a half-day on Saturday. Thus was I at the beginning of a new chapter in my life with high ambitions and expectations. For a brief time all seemed to be coming up roses but all too soon the thorns would make their appearance and this house of cards would come tumbling down.

I was whistling past the graveyard as my past was continuing to haunt me and I knew that eventually I would have to give up the ghost. I was truly leading a double life but decided, unfortunately, to let events run their course, which they did and even more swiftly than I had ever envisioned.

PART FIVE

Regroupment and Reexamination

CHAPTER 10

Graduate School and a Brief

Teaching Interlude

My sense of impending doom was temporarily assuaged by the new regimen my wife and I were undertaking in Fairfield. My full-time course load and full-time employment on campus left me little, if any, time to ruminate about the situation I had put myself in. My wife was busy with her full-time teaching job as well as keeping care of the living quarters in our rented home. We joined a church about two miles from the house and regularly attended Sunday Mass. On a few occasions we also played bingo at the church hall on Friday night. Our main extracurricular activity, however, was usually going to the movies on Friday night and I eagerly looked forward to that respite.

Our lives quickly fell into a set routine and we were both stressed under overly committed schedules. This would be difficult for any couple but for one newly married it was an extra burden we didn't need. This was in October and, looking back, I realize it would have been better if she had followed through with a desire to leave. Also she had gone to see a priest recommended to her by the priest who had married us in New York. He was pastor of a parish about twenty miles away. She then asked me if I would go with her to see him for a counseling session as a possible means of reconciliation. I consented although I had no real expectation that this would be helpful in the long run. We went on a Saturday morning in November and it went well because, even at this late date, I was trying to convince myself that keeping the marriage alive was the right thing to do. This only made the situation worse as I will soon explain. In a spirit of false euphoria, we returned home, went to a movie, "Doctor Zhivago," that night and had intercourse afterwards. It was on that occasion that my wife became pregnant with our son. Thanksgiving rolled around twelve days later and we returned to New York to visit her parents. It was then, on the holiday, that my wife realized how bored I was spending time with her family and must have sensed then that things were on a downhill trajectory.

New Year's and we both went with her parents to a dinner hosted by her sister-in-law's mother. I am sure it must have been suspected that something was wrong but everyone carried on as though all was normal. The next evening her father drove us to the airport as I had to return to work and school. Her father must have known something was afoot but did his best to maintain his composure. I am sure that night that she had a traumatic session with her parents, telling them that we were separated and considering divorce. I didn't feel obliged to tell my family what was happening although I probably should have.

About three days later she called and said she would be returning to Connecticut on January 10. Since I had the car she would of course have to be driven up by her father. I was trying to convince myself that she was coming back to live with me after all but, as I was to soon learn, I was in a state of denial. She arrived in the late morning with her father and uncle in tow, got the keys for the car, and went off to the house, waving goodbye to me as they went. I knew then that she was leaving for good and called the house a number of times but no one answered. Since she didn't come back to pick me up from work I had no recourse but to walk home, a distance of about four miles. When I arrived I found no one home and a "Dear John," or, if you will, "Dear Dick", letter waiting for me. She explained all the reasons why she had to leave and I was again in a state of denial, knowing, but not wanting to admit, that it all had to eventually end like this. Pulling myself together, I walked to and from work over the next two days and then, fortunately, found someone selling a used Chevy station wagon.

The next few weeks passed uneventfully except for a counseling session I had with one of the priests at the University. Nothing was resolved but I felt a little better afterwards. I then worked up enough stamina to call her but that resolved nothing. In the meantime my mother and an old school friend came down to visit and this was a welcome interlude. When our son was born on August 13, a most significant date as I will explain later, I was soon thereafter sent a picture. As time passed I realized that joint custody was not a good idea and just wished to get on with the proceedings, which both lawyers admitted had gone on for too long.

During all this, I completed my graduate studies for my M.A. with the exception of having to write a thesis. I had completed two full semesters as well as a Summer one to earn my 30 credits. The thesis would be worth 6 more. I also needed to obtain gainful employment as my GI Bill would expire once I finished attending the University. I saw a notice at the school that a Religion Teacher was being sought for a girls Catholic High School in White Plains, New York, about a fifty mile drive from Fairfield. I went for the interview just before Easter and was hired shortly thereafter. My thesis was completed and accepted by December of that year. I eagerly anticipated my new job, little knowing what awaited me. I had three strikes against me before even getting started. First of all I had no prior teaching experience, not even cadet teaching, which public schools utilize as a means of testing teacher applicants. Secondly, I was teaching in an all girls school and girls act differently in class when there are no boys present. This would be calamitously exemplified in my freshman class, which, with 34 students, was too large to begin with. Finally I was teaching a subject which wasn't that popular but was, nonetheless, required for graduation. To say the odds were stacked against me would be a gross understatement. I taught classes at all grade levels, Freshman, Sophomore, Junior, and Senior, but the Freshman class was to be my bête-noire. One particular student, whom I remember only as "Susan," seemed to take an intense dislike to me and was a troublemaker with the other girls. When the situation progressed to the point I had to ask the principal to get involved, she was called in for a consultation. She admitted in front of me that she didn't like me but wouldn't say why. It all ended inconclusively with the principal saying she would monitor the situation. I was to learn later from her mother at a parent-teacher conference that the father had previously left the family and Susan hadn't adjusted well to the absence. Possibly I reminded her of her father or maybe she was just in an "anti-male" frame of mind. In either case the problem wasn't resolved and she continued to be a thorn in my side. One day in November the principal walked into the classroom unannounced and found it in its almost habitual state of bedlam. She asked me to leave and then talked to them afterwards. It wasn't long afterwards that she called me to her office to go over the situation. She said she didn't realize how bad it was as I had never asked for help. She also reported that other staff sensed that there was a "sense of mystery" about me. I then felt constrained to tell her the whole morbid tale about my failed marriage and impending divorce. She offered a bit of commiseration and suggested that maybe a co-teaching effort would ameliorate the problem. I, however, sensed that my teaching stint was to be short-lived, seeing what I believed was the proverbial handwriting on the wall. In light of this, I reapplied to the State Department as a backup should I have no other alternative.

All this simmered over the Thanksgiving and Christmas holidays. I flew out to Salt Lake City to spend the Christmas holiday with my twin brother, which was a welcome hiatus indeed. Upon returning to school after New Year's I was notified by the principal that a decision had been made to terminate the contract with the mutual compromise that, if I didn't contest this, the school wouldn't hesitate to recommend me for employment as long as it didn't involve teaching. I realized that this was reasonable not to mention inevitable. My last appearance at the school was to attend a student dance with the students not knowing that I was leaving. That night there was a terrific snowstorm but I headed out anyway and miraculously made it back to Fairfield safe and sound. By now it was just past the middle of January. In addition to my State application, I again took the Civil Service Entrance Exam so I could get on the list for re-employment although I knew that all this would take time and that I needed work in the intermission.

In early February I received notification from New York that my divorce had been finalized. That calamitous chapter in my life had now mercifully ended. I now needed to find some gainful employment as I still had expenses to meet, such as rent, utilities, food, gas, etc. I found temporary employment as an admin assistant working through a temp agency, but it was of a very limited duration. It was at this time, around the middle of the month, that I was called up to New York City for an interview with the Security Division of State at Federal Plaza. It went well and I was assured that I could plan on re-employment when the process had been completed. Then, in March, I secured employment through the Virginia Employment Commission with an outfit called "Zimco," as a sorter and packager at their warehouse of men's clothing to be ultimately distributed to its outlets in-state and well as outside. This outfit would later expand to become what is known today as "Men's Warehouse." It wasn't much of a job but at least it kept me from becoming indigent while again pursuing government employ. I wasn't on the job more than a week when my Chevy was stolen while I was working inside. I could hardly believe it and, after giving a police report, had to walk most of the way home. I called the man who lived upstairs in my rented house and asked him if he could pick me up and he readily agreed. It was at least a fifteen mile distance from Fairfield to Norwalk. When I reported the theft to my insurance agent she said I didn't seem too upset. I mentioned that I lost my job in January, got divorced in February, and now had my car stolen so was somewhat immunized to misfortune. In about three days, with the help of the husband of one of my former co-workers at the University, I bought an old, used car that was at least able to get me around town and paid cash from my remaining reserves.

Around late '73 I was importuned by the local K. of C. council to help them on their Bingo Night and I continued to do this until leaving Connecticut in '75. Anyway, I'm getting a bit ahead of myself.. While working with Zimco I continued communicating with my friend in Saigon, attempting to arrange for her to get a visa to travel to the U.S. Of course that is a lengthy process so didn't expect immediate action. Meanwhile I was in a sort of limbo, being between gainful employment and living very much by myself, pretty much drifting along for the time being.

Around the middle of the year my upstairs renter decided to break his lease and move to South Carolina as he wasn't having much luck with his sales work in Connecticut. I helped him move out and this was known to the landlord. I am sure that this didn't endear me to him but am not sure that was the sole reason my lease wasn't renewed in September. Having been given the required advance notice, I began inquiring around about a suitable alternative. It so happened that someone in the K. of C. Council knew an old woman who was looking to rent her upstairs apartment in her home in Stratford for just $10.00 a week. I naturally jumped at this opportunity and relocated in September. Stratford and Fairfield were on opposite sides of Bridgeport. This turned out to be truly fortuitous as I was laid off from my warehouse job in December just after the Christmas holidays. The reason for the low rent was two-fold. The landlady wanted to have a man in the house as an argument against her daughter who claimed she couldn't live alone in the house. Also, she wanted to have someone to talk to and would often ask me to come down to visit with her when she knew I was at home. This was still a small price to pay for someone now living on unemployment with a car note to pay off.

In the midst of all this, I was informed that my ex-wife had requested an annulment of the marriage. I was sent a questionnaire to be completed as part of the process but gave it no serious consideration as I thought it was unlikely to be approved. In October I had bought a used '68 Ford with only 21,000 miles on it as the old Buick was quickly falling apart. I procured a two year loan through a local bank with the help of the husband of a former co-worker at the University, the same one mentioned previously. He was a vice-president of the bank. The bank was leery about providing the loan as I had no credit history but you have to start somewhere. I could have paid for the car outright from my savings but that would still have left me with no credit history. And so I entered a new year in a state of uncertainty and foreboding.

CHAPTER 11

More Graduate Work and
Government Service

In January of 1975 I was notified by the Diocese of Rochester that my marriage had been annulled. The grounds for the annulment were not given and I was content merely to have closure. Apparently the guidelines for granting these actions are much more liberal than before. In the past it was unheard of to have a marriage annulled which had already been consummated. Even an acquaintance of mine and a leading liberal Catholic theologian, Father Charles Curran, once remarked that the loopholes in granting annulments were large enough to drive a Mack truck through. Be that as it may, I wasn't about to refuse it and took solace in the fact that this chapter in my life was finally over and done with.

It was now necessary to try to cut through the red tape to get my Vietnamese friend into the U.S. Little did I realize it at the moment but this would become critical in just a few more months. Now that I was unemployed, with no good prospects in sight, I also had to decide what alternatives lay before me. I had been informed by the State Department that there was a hiring freeze so that avenue was temporarily closed. It didn't take me long to then focus on pursuing additional graduate work. This seemed to offer many advantages. It would get me off unemployment and allow me to take advantage of GI Bill of rights money to which I was still entitled and, last but not least, would put me back in an environment which I very much enjoyed. To that end I went to the public library and started researching suitable programs. It wasn't long before I took an interest in a Master's program in Guidance and Counseling at Western New Mexico University in Silver City, New Mexico. The subject matter would dovetail well with my previous academic background and there were graduate assistant programs available which also entitled me to in-state tuition, a not inconsiderable bonus. Finally it would get me away from Connecticut, an expensive state to live in even when working, not to mention when unemployed. As I had nothing to lose I requested an application in March and hoped for the best. Concurrently the K. of C. needed someone to do janitorial work part-time and I would have gladly done it but they chose someone else, who was already working full-time. Apparently he had an "in" with the Grand Knight.

Having been living alone for two years I was beginning to feel comfortable in that situation even though I knew that I didn't want it to persist very much longer. In the event it would come to an end in less than a year. Much to my consternation, events in Vietnam were quickly coming to a boil. The communists were rapidly taking control of the North of South Vietnam and working their way South. I knew it was only a matter of time before Saigon fell. This placed me in a state of anxiety since my friend would have to find some way to escape as a refugee or end up trapped in a totalitarian state. I was helpless to do anything and could only hope that she would find a way out in time. I had a brief respite at the end of the month when Easter came as my mother and older brother were visiting New York City for a long weekend. Since I was only about 50 miles away I took a train to New York and joined them for a few days.

Back home again events quickly took on a life of their own. Saigon fell by the end of April and I had no way of knowing my friend's situation. The unemployment situation was so bad that the Unemployment Commission didn't even require that I look for work, only certify that I was still unemployed. Finally everything was done simply by mail and they sent my check every two weeks.

Around the end of May or the beginning of June I received a letter from my friend advising me that she had gotten out of Vietnam and, as a refugee, had been settled in San Jose, California. It seems that, before leaving Vietnam, I had given her my mother's address as a reliable point of contact as a last resort. She had contacted my mother who then gave her my address in Connecticut. To say this was a relief would be a gross understatement. In the meantime I awaited a response to my school application which I had submitted in April. Meanwhile my only social activity was working bingo night at the local K. of C. meeting house.

In June I received notification that I had been accepted by WNMU for classes starting in the Fall. This was exceedingly good news as it now allowed me to have gainful activity for the immediate future. The following month passed uneventfully and by the first week of August I was ready to move. Ironically the K. of C. had asked me if I would take the part-time job as a janitor referred to previously since the man they did hire was proving to be unsatisfactory. I would have gladly accepted it earlier in the year but now I didn't need it. I rented a U-Haul, loaded up my few possessions, and drove up to New York to my mother's house where I could then store what I had and head West to New Mexico.

Upon reflection it seemed that blind fate was working overtime in my favor. When I applied for graduate schooling in New Mexico I didn't know that Vietnam was so near collapse and that my friend would be able to escape before the final takeover by the communists. Now she was domiciled in California, within hailing distance of New Mexico. It seemed we were destined to reunite after that dreadful departure in Saigon more than three years earlier.

I left New York on a Saturday in late August, arriving in Silver City, New Mexico the following Thursday, stopping overnight in Ohio, Illinois, Indiana, Oklahoma, and just across the border into New Mexico. Silver City was at the far end of the state and required a final day of travel. I signed in at the school, was assigned sleeping quarters, and prepared to do the necessary paperwork the following day so I could start classes the next week. The school claimed not to know of a graduate assistantship available to me and also queried as to why I was living in a dormitory at the university. It seems I had mistakenly thought that was my only option and, being informed it wasn't, I searched for an apartment outside and quickly found one only about a mile from WNMU. Then the following Monday I was informed that the school did have an assistantship available to me working for a Dr. Tietze, the head of the music department. This was a commitment of only 4 hours a day, twenty hours a week, and didn't conflict with my classes, which were in the late afternoon or early evening, not unlike my program at Fairfield. In addition I applied and was hired to help Hispanic students with English in the language lab a few hours each week. Everything was, as they say, coming up roses.

To say that New Mexico was a vast contrast to Connecticut would be a gross understatement. To begin with the air was cleaner, the people were friendlier, and the cost of living was certainly lower. I quickly settled into my new routine and looked forward to arranging a meeting with my friend now ensconced in San Jose. She had communicated her phone number to me through my mother and I contacted her a short while after. She was working part-time evenings at an Italian restaurant and going to school in the daytime in an English as a Second Language course. She could get away for about a week in October so I arranged for her to fly from San Jose to Tucson, Arizona which was the nearest major airport to Silver City. In the meantime we talked by phone on the weekends every week. When the day of her arrival came I took off early from my job and drove over to Tucson to await her arrival. I was joyfully expectant yet a bit anxious as we hadn't seen each other in so long. Anyway when she arrived and we embraced it was as though the intervening years melted away in a few brief moments. I drove back to New Mexico, brought her to the apartment, and we proceeded to get re-acquainted.

As is usually the case when one is experiencing joyful moments, the time went all too quickly and, before I knew it, I was taking her back to Tucson for the return flight to San Jose. In the meantime, however, we had decided that I would visit her in San Jose before Thanksgiving and she would then terminate her stay there and relocate with me in New Mexico.

I went back to my routine in Silver City and eagerly anticipated our next get-together.

The weeks flew by and, after finishing my assistantship work on Friday morning, November 21, I set out for San Jose, an overnight trip more than a thousand miles away. I made it to the California border a little past midnight and stayed at a motel in Needles. After only about six hours sleep I started out again as it would be a long drive up highway 5 to San Jose. Getting there around 10 at night I stopped for gas and inquired as to the exact location where my friend lived. As it so happened it was only about a block away. She was most happy to see me but had been a bit stressed out over having to finalize things there knowing she would be leaving with me in a few days and not coming back. The following day we visited with her two friends, an American and his Vietnamese wife, who had recently purchased a home in the suburbs. Two days later we departed San Jose en route to Salt Lake City to spend the Thanksgiving holiday with my twin brother. After an overnight in Elko, Nevada, we arrived in Salt Lake on Wednesday, celebrated Thanksgiving, stayed over one more day, and then left for the return trip to New Mexico. We stopped in Arizona for the night and then set out for Silver city in the morning. In spite of car trouble and emergency repair work, we managed to make it back to Silver City by nightfall.

After resuming my classes, I enrolled my future wife in a program at the local high school that would enable her to get a GED. I then had to plan for the upcoming Christmas holiday as I needed to introduce her to the rest of the family in New York. Our plans were made to fly from Tucson to Rochester, getting there a few days before the big holiday. My mother met us at the airport and everything went well. Our brief visit of about a week had us returning to New Mexico a few days before New Year's. Now I had to get our affairs in order, to include finishing my degree program, arranging for religion instruction in what are referred to as "Cana Conferences" prior to getting married, and, last but not least, planning my post-graduate future..

Everything progressed smoothly and I even obtained, as a source of extra income, part-time weekend work for me and my friend as counselors at a home for what were then referred to as retarded youths. This sort of work can be mentally draining but we got one weekend off a month, which was a most welcome break..

During the Spring break we went to Fort Worth with a Vietnamese couple we befriended in Silver City. They were living in quarters provided by the local parish priest and wanted to visit relatives in Texas. This was a welcome break from the school and work routine in New Mexico.

By happenstance I ran across a "jobs wanted" notice in the University's placement office, seeking someone to fill a communications vacancy at the Navy's BUMED office (Bureau of Medicine and Surgery) in Washington, D.C. This immediately attracted my attention due to my previous communication experience with State. Although it seemed unlikely that a person for the job could not be found in Washington, I figured I had nothing to lose so applied anyway. I had already retaken the Federal Service Entrance Exam and this would simply give me another option.

We planned our wedding for May 8 in San Jose as that was where my soon-to-be-wife had been residing. My M.A. program could be completed by the end of the Summer as I needed only 6 more credit hours. My job prospects looked promising and I had every confidence that something would materialize by the Fall. However, as a default option, I investigated possibly pursuing a third M.A. program at the University of Arizona in Tucson, which would offer me a scholarship and I still had the G.I. bill. This would provide sufficient support until a government job inevitably materialized.

May rolled around quickly and we returned to San Jose for the big day, staying at the home of the couple mentioned previously. The priest officiating at the ceremony had a brief interview with us the day before and mentioned that this was his first time marrying anyone. It was a mixed marriage in more ways than one as my soon to be wife was not a Catholic, but this wasn't seen as a problem. The ceremony was sparsely attended as none of my family were present and that left only some friends and acquaintances my wife made since living in San Jose. The church claimed, however, that it couldn't provide space for the reception afterwards so we held that in the basement, ironically enough, of a Protestant church.

Everything went off as planned and the photographer left us with some very memorable souvenirs. I had asked beforehand if it was permitted to take pictures in church and was told it was "frowned on." That was hardly an obstacle and I proceeded as planned. After a night at the aforementioned couples home, who, incidentally, served as best man and maid of honor, we went to San Francisco the next day. This all-too-brief honeymoon was necessitated by my need to get back to New Mexico to finish up my semester course work.

Within a few weeks, to my immense surprise, I received a letter from the Navy advising me that they were offering the communications position in Washington. As this seemed too good to be true and would necessitate a relocation of some distance, I called to confirm my acceptance and was told that I was being hired because only three other people had applied and all had been disqualified for one reason or another. I would, of course, have to complete my studies elsewhere as I had to start my new employ by the last week of June. I rented a U-haul and we traveled to Virginia in four days, stopping one overnight to visit our friends in Forth Worth.

We anxiously looked forward to this new chapter in our lives, still adjusting to this unexpected stroke of luck. I had come a long way since the last year and, with my new wife, looked forward to a future filled with hope.

CHAPTER 12

Foreign Service Redux

A furnished apartment was found one day after arriving in Northern Virginia, after we stayed overnight at a hotel in Manassas. Our lodgings were only seven miles from my new office, which was located on the outskirts of Washington, opposite my old employer, the State Department, and just across the line from Arlington. I signed a one-year lease with the landlord on Sunday and then reported for work Monday morning.

My work was limited to minor clerical duties for the first six weeks or so as my security clearance had yet to be completed. The fact that I was now married to a Foreign National delayed the procedure beyond the usual processing period. Once I was properly cleared, I was put on my regular midnight shift, working two nights alone and three nights with another civilian.

I quickly settled into the humdrum routine, punctuated outside the office by a first for me, a moving traffic violation. On my way home from work in early August, I was stopped by an Alexandria policeman as he spotted my lack of an inspection sticker. I had planned on getting the car inspected the following weekend, only two days hence, but was issued the ticket anyway. Two days later the car passed inspection but I still had to appear in court on the appointed date of August 13, which also happened to be a Friday. Luckily for me, unlike my wife, I am not superstitious. As I sat in court all the cases before me were adjudicated against the violator. When I appeared in front of the judge I explained that I was planning on getting the car inspected the weekend after the ticket was issued as my work schedule didn't allow me to go on a weekday. When I presented him with proof that the car had indeed passed the required inspection, he dismissed the case without imposing a fine. I left the court exhilarated that I had "won" my case and was somewhat more euphoric that evening than I otherwise might have been. That date had the significance referred to in chapter 10 as it was that night, August 13, that our child was conceived. I did not know it at the time but it was later confirmed by the obstetrician, a Belgian doctor working in Alexandria. Whether this was by mere coincidence or by God's plan, only God knows.

We visited my mother over the Thanksgiving holiday and shared the good news that a grandchild was on the way. The rest of the year passed uneventfully as we spent Christmas at home and looked forward to the new year and an addition to the family. Meanwhile I was growing increasingly restless with my current job, which offered limited promotion possibilities, and decided around March to reapply to the State Department, which, coincidentally, I passed every day on my way to and from work. My name was also still active on the Federal civil service list so I had two potential sources of more gainful employment.

The night of April 30 I went to work as usual and upon arriving was told that I needed to return home immediately as my wife had begun to go into labor. She had contacted an elderly tenant downstairs who took to my wife and looked after her if she needed anything while I was away. I quickly drove to the Alexandria hospital, accompanied by the tenant mentioned above. The obstetrician was called after my wife was admitted and it was shortly determined that the baby could not be delivered naturally, a caesarian procedure being necessary. This upset my wife but, after being convinced that there was no other option, the operation was performed and we became the proud parents of a healthy baby boy. To say this was one of the greatest moments of my life would be an understatement of gargantuan proportions. I rather quickly decided on the names to bestow upon our newborn. He would need Christian names, of course but, with tongue in cheek, I purposely chose names of saints who had recently fallen into some disrepute in the church, there being some recent doubts as to their historicity. Being resentful of this I affirmed my solid belief in them by using them as monikers for our son. I had never heard of saints being "de-sainted," as it were, and decided to go with tradition. This was perceived as a double blessing, having previously lost one son but now gaining another. Who says lightning doesn't strike twice?

My mother came down to visit shortly after the birth and stayed for about a week. This was her first, and, in the event, her only grandchild. The family name had been preserved for at least another generation.

The rest of the year was unnoteworthy and I looked forward to getting adjusted to the new arrival and anticipating any new turn of fortune that would improve our material well being now that the family had grown. At Christmas time I worked part-time as a seasonal employee at a mall not far from our apartment.

The new year saw no change in my job prospects so I decided to work part-time during the day. This was convenient since I worked a steady "graveyard" shift and would always be available to work in the daytime. I applied and was quickly hired as a worker bee at a bank that processed political contributions sent by mail to be forwarded onward. This was menial work, which suited me just fine, as I was just coming off my regular job at the Navy. Also, I was not required to be at the job every day as I was paid an hourly wage only for the time actually worked. It was merely a means of earning a little extra to meet current expenses and wasn't in the least stressful. In fact, there were times when I struggled to stay awake.

By late Summer we were becoming disenchanted with our living quarters as the landlord wasn't providing adequate air-conditioning as our faulty machine wasn't being replaced. I therefore took it upon myself to replace it with an air conditioner from a vacant apartment, which led to a confrontation with the landlord, actually a slumlord, and to my giving him thirty days notice that we were leaving, as required by the lease. This was done without having a clue as to where we would relocate but my luck held true once again. I answered an ad by a family looking to rent the furnished basement of their home at a quite reasonable fee. They were merely wanting to have extra money to pay on the mortgage. We went to see them and an agreement was quickly reached for us to move in early September. Our new lodgings were twelve miles from my job, five miles further than the previous abode, but, believe me, it was well worth it. We had most amicable relations with the homeowners and this would prevail for the fourteen months we lived there. My only regret was that we hadn't found such a living arrangement like that in the first place. We were also closer to shopping as there was a mall less than a mile away to which my wife could walk if she so desired. Also, wonder of wonders, there was a drive-in about a mile away to which we could go and, of course, bring the little one along.

Entering another year I was beginning to wonder when my job applications of long standing would begin to produce any results. As is often the case, in such a situation, when it rains, it pours. I was contacted in early April by U.S. Customs advising me that they wanted to interview me for a position at LAX. I went over to Maryland for the interview and was assured that I would be hired once the red tape had been completed. Not more than a week later, the State Department advised me that they wanted to bring me in for a security interview pursuant to re-hiring me for a Foreign

80

Service assignment. Following up with State, I had my security interview and was told that I could expect a job offer soon. Shortly thereafter I was called by State and offered an assignment following an extensive training course in a new communications program called Afrecone. As the name implies, my assignment would be in Africa and, as it turned out, was to be in Ouagadougou, the capital of what was then referred to as Upper Volta. Having previously considered all the pros and cons as to which job offer to accept, it was a no-brainer, in view of my past experience with State, overtime compensation, government-paid living quarters and, last but not least, my starting salary.

So here I was off again to see the world, but accompanied this time by my new family. In the meantime my wife was finishing being processed for naturalization, which, fortuitously, was completed just a few weeks before we left for Africa.

We arrived uneventfully in Ouagadougou around the 10th of November and were ensconced in a roomy house in an area known at the Zone du Bois. After a brief breaking-in period I quickly acclimated to my new surroundings both at home and at work. My wife was relieved of the boredom that could accompany such an assignment by being occupied at home with the care of our still relatively young son. One of the most memorable features of the capital city was its large downtown Catholic cathedral, a hallmark of French colonial rule. Our two-year stint was punctuated by a welcome R and R midway through the tour, which we enjoyed back home. During this time a coup took place in Upper Volta but, other than that, the tour was uneventful.

As was the m.o. in the Foreign Service a so-called "hardship" tour was followed by a "plum" one, so to speak. This certainly proved to be the case when my onward assignment was Brussels, Belgium. This proved to be most memorable for its civilian as well as military advantages, there being a NATO PX and Commissary about 50 miles away, which was reachable by military bus leaving from the American DOD school. I had only to drop my wife off and then pick her up afterwards. Our son also began pre-school at a Belgian facility and then entered first grade at the American School. Not surprisingly, family members were eager to visit us and my mother and older brother were the first to do so during our first Summer there. Another visit was made in the Fall of the following year, again by my mother, but accompanied this time by my twin brother and his wife. Although I had a used car to get around town, Brussels had a superb metro system which was useful not only to get to the embassy but for recreational purposes as well. I was allowed to extend my tour four months due to the need for our son to complete his school year and then take what is referred to as "home leave" in time to deploy to my next assignment.

As was to be expected the next assignment would not be so pampering but New Delhi was undeniably better than a West African posting. We arrived there in mid-August and were taken to our temporary quarters, just across the street from the embassy by our sponsor, the designated individual assigned to get us settled. He would, as it turned out, become a lifelong friend of mine. After about four months we moved into our permanent housing, which was larger than what we previously had. Our son entered second grade at the American School but was struggling to keep up. His mother tongue being more Vietnamese than English, as well as his time in a Belgian school were proving obstacles difficult to overcome. After plodding through the second grade it was decided that it would be better for him to repeat the second year rather than continue trying to keep up. In this endeavor a speech therapist was also enlisted to help the process along. My wife overreacted to this seeing it as some sort of "failure," but it proved to be the proper choice. Unsurprisingly, there were no family visits during the India assignment. This was compensated for by the option of taking an R&R back to the U.S. in the Summer of '86. Meanwhile, we found the assignment pleasant enough to request a one-year extension, making it a three-year tour rather than a two-year one. It was further highlighted by Pope John Paul II's visit in 1986, a truly memorable experience. I also had an opportunity to see much of the country as I was assigned tdy, at various times, to all three of our consulates, which were then known as Bombay, Madras, and Calcutta. Our son progressed satisfactorily through the third grade as the assignment came to an end in mid-year of 1987.

Unexpectedly an assignment opened up in Ankara, Turkey which I applied for and obtained. This seemed to be a good compromise between a "hardship" tour and a "choice" one, if you will. It turned out to be one of the best Foreign Service choices I ever made. The embassy was a medium-size operation, unlike the factory atmosphere of a Brussels, or the constraining style of a Ouagadougou. Also, it offered a DOD school which would serve our son well, getting him through the mid elementary fourth, fifth, and sixth grades. For my wife there was also the Air Force base only about a 15 minute drive away, which housed a PX, Commissary, Non-Com Officers Club, library, movie theater, as well as the school our son attended. As a member of NATO, these facilities were available in Turkey. Looking back, unclouded by nostalgia, I can assure you, this posting was the most enjoyable for us all. Attendance at Catholic Mass was available at the Vatican Embassy, a short ride from our apartment. As with India, I requested and got a one-year extension to what was a two-year deployment.

Having made a very wise choice with the aforementioned I then proceeded to make a very imprudent one in the aftermath. My last supervisor in Turkey was stationed in Riyadh, Saudi Arabia and often talked up its merits. Unfortunately it had more demerits for me but I didn't realize that until it was too late. I hazard to suggest that a tour in a Communist country would have been more tolerable. There is nothing worse, I submit, than a theocratic state, especially when it's religion is not yours. We had to attend religious services at the embassy presided over by a chaplain who snuck in incognito. On the upside, our son was able to attend the American School and finish his elementary education. Also, the quite new embassy was conducive to a pleasant working environment. What will be remembered most, of course, was the evacuation of unnecessary dependents, to wit, my wife and son among others, during the Gulf War, something, of course, which I could not have foreseen when I accepted the assignment. Fortunately this was of only three months duration and after an R&R back home, I retrieved them and returned to complete my assignment. Due to the trauma of this event, I next resolved to take a domestic assignment with State and put down some permanent roots, such as buying a house so that my family would have a domicile should such a situation arise in the future. We returned in August 1992, in time to start my new job just after Labor Day and for our son to begin high school in Stafford, Virginia.

PART SIX

Bread and Circuses

CHAPTER 13

The Knights:

A Veritable Money Machine

K of C, which, if pronounced too rapidly, might sound like "KFC," would, I submit, put any franchise, bar none, to shame with its obsessive propensity to amass donations, whenever and wherever the situation arises. I believe it never met a fundraiser it didn't like.

I first joined the Knights in 1966 (see chapter 7) while I was still in the Army and have been a member now for 48 years. There wasn't a council at Fort Gordon, Georgia that I can recall so, for the time-being, I was simply a card-carrying member of the fraternity. Actually this was to continue to be the case as I entered the State Department Foreign Service just three months after leaving the military. To the best of my recollection, the Knights have chapters in thirteen countries outside the U.S. and I never served in any of them. They are Canada, the Philippines, Mexico, Poland, the Dominican Republic, Puerto Rico, Panama, the Bahamas, the Virgin Islands, Cuba, Guatemala, Guam and Saipan. I was able to take an active role in a K. of C. Council during my time in Connecticut (see chapters 10 and 11), while living in Fairfield and then Stratford, which were on opposite sides of Bridgeport.

Bingo night at the Fairfield Council home was a perennially reliable money-maker, but it wasn't the only game in town. After the bingo was over, a small group of poker players convened for rounds of cutthroat poker. Knowing they were much more skilled at this than I, I studiously avoided getting involved. I don't know how much money changed hands but can be reasonably certain that it was more than nickels and dimes. Even though, while living on unemployment, I was unable to earn a few extra dollars, about fifty dollars a week doing janitorial labor at the council home, due to my not having an "in" with the Grand Knight, I continued volunteering with bingo until leaving Connecticut. However, except for a brief stint as membership director from 1976-1977, while living in Alexandria, I would never again volunteer for service with the Knights. My position as a membership director was short-lived as I failed to entice new members to join. I wasn't able to sell others on the benefits of becoming a Knight, not only perhaps because I wasn't totally convinced myself of the merits of joining, but also because of my lack of aggressiveness when it comes to selling anything. If there is anything the K. of C. values above all else it is salesmanship. One instance that sticks in my memory while in Alexandria was the sudden death of one of the older members. At the funeral home, the grand knight dispensed with the saying of the rosary, suggesting that we could pray the rosary at home in memory of the deceased. Didn't the motto of "fraternity" merit a public display of prayer for a long-standing member? I kept my membership active with the Alexandria Council even after settling in Stafford, Virginia, after working overseas for thirteen years. This maneuver kept me unobligated to the Stafford Council, as I was not a member, as well as to the Alexandria counterpart, as I lived too far away to be of practical benefit to them. A truly Machiavellian operation if ever there was one. I had been taken advantage of once and I was determined not to let it happen again. Which brings to mind the old cliché, "first time shame on them, second time shame on you." I can truthfully say I didn't miss the fraternal or fellowship aspect since I didn't find much of it present among the members I knew in Connecticut and Virginia. My usefulness in the seemingly endless pursuit of raising money appeared to be all that mattered.

I must admit, however, that there was an upside to my association with the K. of C., namely their insurance programs. Their insurance headquarters is located in New Haven, Connecticut, where, incidentally, the K. of C. was founded on March 29, 1882 by Father Michael McGivney, currently on the path to sainthood. Being the third largest fraternity in the world, they have a captive clientele and are able to offer insurance, whole life only, as well as long-term health care at extremely competitive rates. Some members have openly admitted that they joined the Knights primarily due to the insurance benefits, not so they could volunteer in the many fund-raising activities in which the K. of C. engages. I found the long-term care option to be especially beneficial, not for me but for my wife. Playing the odds that most women live longer than their spouses and outnumber men in nursing homes by a ratio of about 9 to 1, I obtained coverage for my wife only. Also, with my family history in mind as to the longevity of the male side - I don't recall any who lived into advanced old age - and the demise of the few I am familiar with could be said to have died in a heartbeat, so to speak. It's a gamble I admit, but then a lot of things in life are a gamble so you just have to play the odds and hope you come out a winner.

The Knights pride themselves as being a charitable organization and, apparently, are firm believers in the old adage that charity begins at home. The K. of C. is protected from federal tax by its status as a church charitable organization Their insurance program is joined cheek by jowl to the Vatican Bank, whose finances are anything but transparent. The Supreme Knight's salary was estimated as recently as 2011 as somewhere North of 1.5 million dollars. It isn't clear if that includes such gratuities as a limo, jet, villa in Rome, etc., not to mention his salary as one of the four board members overseeing the Vatican Bank. I submit that a miniscule number of Catholic laity, not to mention the members themselves, is aware of the generous perks associated with being a Supreme Knight. Could not some of this money be more usefully given to the aid of the poor? Sound familiar?

Then there is the involvement of the Knights in political matters. With this in mind, I can conjecture that Pope John Paul II didn't carelessly call the K. of C. the "strong right arm of the church." In 2010 the Knights poured millions of dollars into the Minnesota gubernatorial race in opposition to the Democratic candidate due to, among other things, his position on same-sex marriage. In spite of their best efforts, the Democrat won in a very tight race. Again could this money not have been more profitably given in aid to the poor and suffering? How the organization sidesteps the IRS regulation 501(c) (3) in this regard is beyond my comprehension. I am sure that this is only the tip of the iceberg as to how involved the Knights are in political matters, but it suffices to get the point across.

This, of course, is not to deny that the Knights do perform many charitable benefits in support of the needy. One that readily comes to mind is the tootsie role drive that is conducted around the country by every parish that has a K. of C. Council. Being politically correct it no longer uses the "r" word in soliciting donations but refers to its benefactors as the "mentally challenged" or some such euphemism. Also of some note are the blood drives it sponsors in support of the Red Cross at parish centers around the U.S. Then, of course, there are the pancake breakfasts as well as the bingo games mentioned previously, all supposedly for charitable ends. Also let's not forget the Christmas card drive every December and the Super Bowl promotions in February. The Alexandria, Virginia Council of which I am a member, having joined in 1976, is big-time into bingo, whereas, oddly enough, my local Stafford Council doesn't engage in this proven money-maker at all. I have heard various excuses ranging from the pastor doesn't condone gambling to the stealing of bingo winnings by volunteers when the game was sponsored. Actually, a pastor who was stationed here as recently as 1999, had decided to resurrect bingo and had even applied for a license from the state to do so. However, before this could be finalized, he was transferred and his successor never followed up on it. This is a rare instance of the Knights passing up a good and reliable source of income. A most rare omission I would suggest.

Then there is the ceremonial aspect of membership. This is particularly prominent at church celebrations during Christmas and Easter, not to mention funerals of deceased "brothers." The Knights at the fourth degree, the highest possible, dress in their plumed hats, capes, and, with their accompanying swords, make a memorable impression. Although eligible for the fourth degree, I never saw the worthiness of attaining it merely to engage in such formal activities and have been quite content with my third degree status.

Not surprisingly the Knights have fallen victim to the modern day tendency of young people not to be joiners. Their membership rolls suffer depletion with the demise of those on the rolls, whether active or inactive, without the commensurate filling of the void with new membership. I am sure that such fraternities such as the Masons, the Elks, and the American Legion are suffering the same fate. This was vividly brought home to me at my local parish when a neighbor of mine, a born-again Knight, if you will, tried to cajole me into joining the parish council. That he would need the services of someone my age in a reasonably populated council for a relatively small church speaks volumes. For the reasons mentioned above I refused to take the bait.

Admittedly my State Department career, requiring me to live in places where I could not maintain active membership, loosened my ties to the organization. Yet, in view of what has been mentioned above, I believe those ties would have been tenuous at best in any event. This brings to mind another instance where "fraternity" failed to be an asset, at least for me. When I was stationed back at the Department in 1996 for my only domestic assignment, an opening came up for a supervisory position in the main communications center. My former boss in Switzerland, working there and knowing that the hiring officer was also a Knight, advised him that I also was a member, believing that this would make me a shoo-in for the job. This, however, proved not to be the case as, apparently, someone else had more of an "in" than I did. Thus, for me, history repeated itself, ability and availability not being determining factors. Fortunately, in this instance, it did not result in my not having a job, just not having the one I preferred.

Unbeknownst to many, I am sure, is the role the Knights played in keeping the John Paul II Center in D.C. afloat as it teetered on the brink of insolvency. The former pope may be referred to as "great" in a pr gambit but, obviously, his star appeal has faded and he isn't that "great" an attraction for the faithful in the years following his papacy. The K. of C. donated millions of dollars to keep the Center profitable, which has also now gotten an extra infusion of notoriety with John Paul's April canonization. The K. of C. seems to have an open checkbook for causes it deems worthy of its support, whether political or religious.

Either by divine providence or simply coincidence, only God knows, almost all of my active participation with the K. of C. has taken place, appropriately, in Connecticut, which is the state of its birth. In view of all that has been elaborated above, I look with a jaundiced eye at any solicitations received from the Knights, rightfully suspicious of where my donations are really ending up. Ironically my membership will prove more beneficial after my demise than while I lived, due to the windfall my wife will receive in insurance benefits, even though, even more ironically, she can't even be a member.

CHAPTER 14

A Reactionary Turn to the Right, Religiously and Politically

There was a time, not that long ago, when the Catholic Church appeared to be somewhat left of center, both politically and religiously. It seemed to have an unmistakable bias with the Democrats, it being the only major party to nominate a Catholic for president, doing so in 1928, 1960, and, most recently, in 2004 with the nominations of Al Smith, John Kennedy, and John Kerry, respectively. Even more recently, the country has elected its first Catholic Vice-President in the person of Joe Biden. A Democrat.

Political influence upon Catholics presented itself forcefully through Tammany Hall, which was founded in the late 18th century and endured until just past the middle of the 20th century. Noted mainly for its graft and corruption, the organization nonetheless was noteworthy for coming to the aid of immigrants, notably the Irish, who arrived in America following the potato famine back home in the mid-eighteenth century. There was also a sizable representation among the Italians, the last forceful leader of Tammany being Carmine DeSapio. Politicians in New York had to contend with Tammany Hall, knowing that their fates would rise or fall depending on Tammany's influence. When New York was a powerful voting bloc in the Electoral College, Tammany's political clout was an outsize factor. When immigration swelled the ranks of Tammany's benefactors, many of these being Catholics, the so-called "Catholic vote" truly did exist and was of significant advantage to the Democratic Party. In the nineteenth century many Germans also migrated to the U.S., perhaps half of whom were Catholic as opposed to the Irish, who were almost all Catholic.

Of course, as the country expanded Westward, migrants followed so that newly arrived Catholics could be found in ever-increasing numbers beyond the Mississippi. The Democrats, being a quarter-century older than the Republicans, were in good position to attract the allegiance of these newcomers in major metropolitan centers, such as New York, Philadelphia, Boston, and New York. The Republicans were not helped by the distinct impression that they were a party predominantly of white, anglo-saxon Protestants, know pejoratively as WASPs. Even today, African-Americans are overwhelmingly Democrat, although the first Republican president, Abraham Lincoln, is fondly remembered by them as having freed the slaves.

Perhaps the Catholic-Democrat alliance reached its crescendo with the election of President Kennedy in 1960. Since then it has been eroded by, among other things, the breaking away of the so-called "solid South" from the Democrats into the firm grip of the Republicans. As a voting bloc Catholics became less predictable and loosened their ties with the Democratic Party. As will be discussed in more detail in the remainder of this chapter, voters were seen as being more ideological, identifying themselves as "liberal" or "conservative," these divisions being represented in both parties. The more recent rise of "independents" has further diminished membership in either major party.

In what can be viewed as a bit of hypocrisy, the Republican Party gives lip service respecting its opposition to contraception and abortion and then does nothing substantive to change the status quo once it gains political victory. The Democrats at least are consistent with their views and subsequent actions upon gaining office.

Catholics, once thought to be safely within the domain of the party - read Democrat - dispensing social safety nets, Social Security and Medicare coming quickly to mind, were being increasingly influenced by moral issues. As wedge issues those of abortion and birth control have quickly come to the forefront. What with the papal encyclical Humanae Vitae of 1968 and the Roe v. Wade Supreme Court decision of 1973, the religious and secular lines of battle were drawn. These landmark events, in the religious and secular realms respectively, have minimal chances of being reversed any time soon, particularly the former. Unfortunately, both issues have been shamelessly politicized in a country supposedly sworn to uphold the principle of separation of church and state enunciated by the founding fathers.

The Republican Party has taken up the cudgels and placed itself on the side of those opposing abortion, the so-called "right to lifers," a misnomer I would submit, as well as those against birth control. With the Democrats identified with the "pro choice" element in the abortion debate as well as the condoners of contraception, the Catholic Church has found a new home within the Republican Party. If there is such an entity as the "Catholic vote," which, I submit, is highly debatable, then it would appear that the Republican Party should have a lock on it. Yet this can be countermanded by the seemingly large number of so-called Democrats who vote for candidates who do not support the Catholic Church's positions on birth control or abortion, to name a few. Obviously there is a divide between the hierarchy and the laity on many social issues and this appears, if anything, to be widening. Our first Catholic vice-president, Joseph Biden, is admittedly pro-choice and yet considers himself a faithful Catholic, even mentioning that he prays the rosary daily and is a regular communicant.

The issue of capital punishment, a prime example of doctrinal change, has seen an about-face with the Catholic Church. Once not so long ago it supported capital punishment, asserting that the State, in taking a person's life, was acting for God. Then, by the late '70's or so, the church stood opposed to capital punishment, apparently as a bulwark to it's "pro-life" stance as exemplified most stridently on the subject of abortion. Then the question arises, if the church can change its position on one issue, why not on others? The logical answer, of course, is that it can. When the contraception matter was being seriously debated in the '60's, a papal panel of laymen and clergy was assigned to study the matter and a majority concluded that a liberalization of the doctrine was in order. However, Pope Paul VI, oft times referred to as the "Hamlet Pope", was of mixed feelings on the matter, until he was influenced by the then Cardinal Wojtyla, later Pope John Paul II, asserting that a change could not be allowed. Precedent had been established by Pope Pius XI in Casti Connubii, and should not be overturned. Thus came about Humanae Vitae in 1968, which reaffirmed the church's stance against contraception,and the disastrous fallout which ensued with many theologians. priests and laity, objecting. The reverberations are still being felt to this day.

A very modern phenomenon of a hard right turn with respect to church-state issues plays out in the current Supreme Court, where you have four conservative justices, including the Chief Justice, and a "swing" justice, who usually votes with the conservative bloc, who are Catholic and have all been appointed by Republican presidents. This would give the impression, rightfully so, I would submit, that the Republican Party is hand in glove with the Catholic Church on a whole array of social issues and defends the conservative view. This liberal-conservative tension has become even more pronounced with the election of Barack Obama in 2008, manifesting itself no more prominently than in the contraceptive clause in the Affordable Care and Patient Protection Act passed in 2010. The matter of protecting one's conscientious beliefs against the dictates of government has become a can of worms, forcing the government to grant religious exceptions and to work out compromises involving third party actors in the debate. No amount of compromise, however, appears to satisfy the Catholic hierarchy, although the vast majority of the Catholic faithful accept contraception as a necessary evil, if you will, if, in fact, they consider it evil at all. The Church's opposition to contraception only exacerbates the abortion issue since it facilitates that situation among those who don't or won't practice birth control. In a final irony, the producer of the birth control pill was none other than Dr. John Rock. One might even say that the Catholic Church was between a Rock and a hard place (double entendre intended).

The Catholic Church has taken a far right turn with the ascendancy of rightist offshoots within the church, none more prominent than the secretive offspring Opus Dei, founded in 1928 by a devotee of fascist dictator Francisco Franco. It has been frequently characterized as "neo-fascist," an appellation which, I submit, is right on target. From its founding in the late '20's until its emergence as a power player in the late to early '70's, it attracted little publicity but has now emerged as a prominent mover in Catholic affairs.

Its founder, Father Jose Maria Escriva de Balaguer, was canonized in 2002, just 27 years after his death in 1975, in what might possibly be considered a rush to judgment, giving the organization a patina of respectability it never previously had. With meeting houses all over the world and a massive multi-million dollar headquarters on Madison Avenue in New York City, it has entrenched itself in secular society, which it nonetheless desires to hold at arm's length.

Claiming membership among the clergy and lay celibates (supernumeraries) as well as the general non-celibate laity (numeraries), it has made significant stealthy inroads within the Catholic Church, many of its members holding positions of prominence within Catholicism. The former director of the Vatican Press Office for Pope John Paul II, Joaquin Navarro-Valls, was a card-carrying member, although John Paul himself was not. In the secular realm, the former director of the FBI, Louis Freeh, is also a prominent acolyte, if you will. There is a parish in Great Falls, Virginia, Saint Catherine of Siena, within the Arlington Diocese, that proudly advertises itself as an Opus Dei church. It has been variously described as "rich, powerful, and corrupt" Be that as it may, Opus Dei also has the singular distinction of having been granted the status of a private prelature, a unique privilege given to an organization, endowing it with the ability to operate as an autonomous entity within the Church.

I have experienced Opus Dei up close and personal as my parish of St. William of York in Stafford, Virginia has had at least two and, probably, three Opus Dei clergy assigned to it in the last 13 years. This is somewhat remarkable as Opus Dei clergy supposedly comprise only 2% of the entire Catholic clergy. The first such clergyman openly displayed his allegiance by publishing little aphorisms in the weekly bulletin, which were taken from sayings in "The Way," written by the founder referred to above. To me it all appeared analogous to sayings or quotes from Ben Franklin's "Poor Richard's Almanac," or dare I say it, from Chairman Mao's "Little Red Book." Suffice it to say I have had a most unexpected and, for me, unwelcome, introduction to this largely secret organization, which, even in today's seemingly well-educated and informed society, is not all that well known.

Other organizations worthy of mention include the Catholic League for Religious and Civil Rights, founded in the U.S. in 1973, The Society of St. Pius X (Lefebvrists), founded in France in 1970 by Father Marcel Lefebvre, Communion and Liberation, founded in Italy in 1954 by Don Luigi Giussani.

These aforementioned organizations, being active in such diverse countries as Spain, France, Italy and the U.S., exemplify the wide-ranging scope of the Catholic Church's move to the right. Yet most of it is happening under the unwatchful eye of the layman in the pew.

Shortly before his death, the late Cardinal Carlo Martini commented that the Church was 200 years behind the times -- just about in step with the Napoleonic era. The late cardinal was liberal by Catholic Church standards and he was widely respected and even considered as a possible pope. Martini was concerned about declining attendance and confidence in the church by its members and worried that official Catholic policy was alienating its followers. I would be much less judgmental and submit that the Church is only about 50 years behind the times.

CHAPTER 15

Sex Scandals and Cover-Ups

The storm clouds had been gathering for a long time but no one in authority appeared to want to take them seriously until, that is, they could no longer be ignored. The National Catholic Reporter revealed that as far back as the mid-'80's, the Catholic Church had been advised of incidents of clerical pedophilia that had not been investigated and subsequently adjudicated. This was the proverbial calm before the storm, waiting for the dam to burst. All the ingredients were there for a perfect storm but the church chose to hide its head in the sand. In an effort to avoid any scandals that might ensue, suspect clergy were moved from parish to parish or, on less frequent occasions, sent to St. Luke's Institute in Silver Spring, Maryland where it was thought they could be rehabilitated. Another alternative has been to place clerical pedophiles in environments where they face minimal temptations, ministering to the elderly, other retired clergy, etc. All this, in the final event, amounted to a virtual kicking of the can down the road, if you will, until the dam finally burst at the dawn of the 21st century. The chickens were coming home to roost and when they did it was with an unholy vengeance, if you will.

Of course the sex scandal was not the first and assuredly will not be the last to mar the reputation of the Catholic Church. However, it is far and away the biggest and the most difficult to contain by damage control and, ultimately, coverups. Some pundits have gone so far as to opine that the sex abuse revelations have caused more harm to the Catholic Church since anything since the Protestant Reformation itself. Such an open-ended assertion is matter for a whole other debate, or series of debates, and is certainly not within the purview of this modest literary endeavor. As much as people may be repulsed by the actions themselves, they are even more alienated, I submit, by the ensuing cover-ups.

The Catholic Church has always been proud of its stellar reputation as a staunch defender of morality and ethical exceptionalism and rightly so, I might attest. Yet when it appears to go to any lengths, lawful or otherwise, to protect that reputation, it invariably has the opposite effect of demeaning it. No institution or individual, secular or religious, should be above the law. To the contrary, religious institutions should be paradigms of virtue and strict adherence to the law, not only of the state but, above and beyond, that of God. In this most abominable abuse of moral authority and ethical standards, the Catholic Church has lost the moral high ground and will be a long time regaining it if, in fact, it ever truly does.

The emphasis during this cataclysm has been focused primarily on how to deal with the effects and, hopefully, staunch the bloodletting. Thus the "zero tolerance" position taken by the conference of bishops in Dallas and the removal of priests from active ministry once credible charges have been brought by the secular authorities. These are definitely moves in the right direction but they are insufficient, dealing only with the symptoms and not also with the causes of the disease itself. Of course, that opens up a whole Pandora's box of questions as to the influence of an all-male celibate clergy, the presence of homosexuals, ephebophiles, and pedophiles in the priesthood, the insufficient psychological screening of candidates for the priesthood, etc. These are matters that must eventually be dealt with but will require extensive research and objective discussion by recognized periti before they can be properly and effectively addressed. Meanwhile, the spreading cancer of clerical sex abuse must be put into remission, if you will, and the damage kept to as minimal a level as possible.

It is understandable that the Church would want to minimize the collateral damage but, in its compulsion to preserve the Church's standing in the eyes not only of the faithful but, I submit, but also of those of other faiths, not to mention the secular world at large, it has only further poisoned the well, if you will. At my local parish, I heard a priest attest from the pulpit that only one percent of the clergy has been guilty of sex abuse. This assertion can be easily refuted in the present day world of mass communication. Even the WCCB (World Council of Catholic Bishops) has admitted that the percent of such violators is between 6-8 percent. What reason would they have to inflate the number? The old adage that honesty is the best policy still holds true. To pretend otherwise is simply to insult people's intelligence and further betray their trust.

A most blatant attempt at a cover-up was the case of Cardinal Bernard Law of Boston. Apparently he considered himself above the law, if you will, until, that is, he was threatened with being subpoenaed to appear before the civil authorities referent to instances of sex abuse committed by clergy in his own archdiocese. It was then that the Vatican itself intervened and appointed him to a safe sinecure within the Holy See, thus giving him diplomatic immunity from prosecution, this being done at the instigation of the Pope himself. Others, unfortuitously, in the name of justice at least, have not been nearly so fortunate. To my own chagrin, I have gone to school with some of these abusers and, if not, am acquainted with a few others.

Viewed in its proper context, this situation is not of a modern dimension, as it has existed within the religious and secular world since human interaction began, which is, of course, to say for a very long time. It may have been exacerbated in the Church with the introduction of mandatory celibacy by the late twelfth century. I was not even aware of this until I was almost forty years old and I attended Catholic schools for twenty years. I would imagine that an extremely high percentage of the faithful is not aware of it to this present day. It is one of the best kept secrets in the Catholic Church. Of course by admitting it the Church would be opening a veritable can of worms as the laity would then ask why it could not be changed back to its original status of non-celibacy. And, trust me, the Church does not want to go there. However, I digress.

As should be manifestly apparent by now, we have a multi-faceted problem here and there is no silver bullet to deal with it. The Church must, nonetheless, contend with the matter at hand as best it can and then undertake the long-term solutions, which, I submit, are available if only the Church has the will and determination to implement them. The plague of sex abuse cannot, of course, be thoroughly eliminated, but it can certainly be confronted and kept under as much control as is humanly possible, not to mention spiritually required.

Not wishing to rub the Church's nose in this debacle, yet wishing to bring transparency to an all-too-secret world of sex abuse and cover-ups, the story doesn't end with the abuse of minors. While less sensational and prominent in the news, there have been instances of clergy impregnating willing or unwilling women and then coercing them into obtaining abortions. Then there are the not-to-be-talked-about situations of clergy having intercourse with each other, some being even of a high rank and thus intimidating their consensual or non-consensual intimates, as the case may be. Of course we don't even want to broach the cases of clergy having illicit relations with lovers and then leaving the priesthood without applying for laicization. Such permission is rarely granted, the main concern of the church being that disrepute not be brought upon the Church, thus encouraging such individuals to lead covert lives so as not to scandalize the faithful. I am familiar myself with situations of this sort and can feel only compassion for these "excommunicated" individuals, which is much more, I submit, than the hierarchy is willing to show. However, with a more open-minded papacy and the pressure of public opinion, the possibilities of "de-excommunication" exist and have, in fact been used on a few rare occasions in other matters, even under the tutelage of Pope Benedict XVI, not exactly the poster boy for reform and liberalization.

Then there have been instances, although extremely rare, of clergy committing homicide and, not quite so rare, of driving under the influence and committing vehicular manslaughter. All dirty laundry, however, is not able to rise to the level of a juicy sex scandal. Unfortunately for the Church, not to mention the individuals involved, nothing so rivets the attention of the public so much as a sex scandal. In the Church's defense it should be pointed out that instances of sex abuse perpetrated by non-Catholic clergymen as well as public servants such as school coaches and teachers, except on rare occasions, do not get as much sensational print coverage. However, the Church itself is partly to blame for this as it has always put itself on a pedestal, above the shortcomings and violations that are commonplace in what it commonly refers to as the wicked outside world. This has magnified its transgressions beyond a point that they may not deserve.

The National Catholic Reporter, an independent Catholic newspaper, has been an indispensable source of information on this matter. Then there are the Boston Globe, the New York Times, and the Washington Post, which have kept the reading public abreast of developments in this scandal. The Globe, which originally broke the story, has been especially conscientious in reporting the twists and turns in this evolving nightmare. Not unexpectedly, the Church has cried "foul," but I know of no instance where any of these publications has been successfully sued for libel in the civil courts. In the court of public opinion they haven't fared any better. The initial reports proved to be only the tip of the iceberg as more and more credible accusations of sexual abuse came to light, some stretching back as much as forty years or more. Not surprisingly, people came forward trying to take financial advantage of the situation by making false accusations, claiming "repressed memory," as a rationale for not coming out sooner.

The financial repercussions have become so great that at least seven U.S. dioceses have declared bankruptcy after their insurance policies refused to cover such exigencies. The monetary cost in the U.S. has been conservatively estimated as exceeding one billion dollars and counting. Many cases have been settled out of court by offering financial settlements to the victims and their families. However, I believe that the spiritual cost, while less tangible, will be even greater. Some have left the Church, never to return, while others, myself included, have incurred an irreparable wound to their faith and trust in the Catholic priesthood.

To make matters worse, this is a scandal whose timeline is undefined. Just when the scandal appears to have abated, more cases come forth. The best the Church can hope for, it seems to me, is a holding action or an uneasy truce while attempting to resolve this dilemma as satisfactorily as possible. Giving more than lip service to the victims of sexual abuse is, I submit, a most necessary and unavoidable first response if the healing is to substantially begin. I see tentative movements in this direction,but much more needs to be done on a person-to-person basis such as papal meetings with survivors of those abused by priests. Perhaps there is light at the end of this very long tunnel if only we do not lose faith and do not submit to despair. The jury is still out.

Chapter 16

Reflection and Reassessment

To declaim that my spiritual journey over the past nearly seventy years has been a torturous and complicated odyssey would be a gross understatement. To depart from one's initial environment, upbringing, and training cannot be an easy one under even the best of circumstances. Yet such departures have been made by many in an almost peremptory manner without ever looking back. That has not been the case for me as I continue to look backward and forward like the two-headed Janus for whom the year's first month in the Gregorian calendar is named. Thus the nomenclature for this chapter, which encompasses both reflection and reassessment.

As an "ism" among many, I have found "Catholicism" to contain inconsistencies and contradictions which it so readily attributes to other ideologies as it may suit its purposes at any given time. Prominent among them at the present time is it's canonization process, whereby individuals are declared saints, having attained the goal of heaven in God's eternal presence. Such a procedure in times past was quite methodical and even, one might say, adversarial in its use of what was termed a "devil's advocate" in the process leading up to sainthood. It was not uncommon for the time span from initiation to culmination to encompass decades, or even centuries. Now we have the most recent phenomenon of a saint, to wit Pope John Paul II, being canonized within the short span of nine years. Not only that but he himself canonized more individuals than all his predecessors combined, a virtual assembly line of saints one might say. The bar has also been considerably lowered with John Paul II and John XXIII being counted among the ranks of the sainted after verification of only two miracles and one miracle respectively. The long standing minimum before was three verifiable miracles. There is also the unseemly lobbying among powerful groups to get their candidates canonized. A blatant example of this affords itself in the canonization of Father Jose Maria Escriva de Belaguer, the founder of Opus Dei, an ultra conservative prefecture in the Catholic Church. His road to sainthood was traversed in only twenty-seven years, it having been culminated in 2002 after his death in 1975. People are being rushed to this supreme honor as a means of meeting an agenda or so it would appear. The dual canonizations of 2014 were precedent-setting and were necessitated, all objections notwithstanding, by the apparent need to make the bitter pill of John Paul II's inclusion easier to swallow with the accompanying aloe of good Pope John's addition to the rolls of the sainted. What the future will bring one can only imagine. There are even rumors of sainthood being extended to Dorothy Day and Thomas Merton, so perhaps there is hope for the Church after all.

Overlooked in modern history is the selectivity the Catholic Church uses when exercising the punishment of excommunication. Many lay people might incur such a status merely by being a member of such an organization as "Call to Action," or "We are Church," liberal outgrowths, which actually occurred in the Lincoln, Nebraska diocese of now-retired Bishop Fabian Bruskewitz. On the contrary, the Catholic Church never excommunicated Mussolini or Hitler, both Catholics, who committed far greater offenses, apparently because it would have been inopportune to do so. Where is the justice in that? Not only that but Popes Pius XI and Pius XII willingly collaborated with Mussolini and Hitler respectively. Apparently the rules are to be enforced only when it is convenient for the Church to do so. This has been exemplified on a much smaller scale at my parish church where, at Christmas Eve Mass, the priest, who happened to be Opus Dei, announced most solemnly before distributing communion that only card-carrying Catholics in good standing can receive the host. Yet we had the instance reported in the media of a Catholic priest elsewhere allowing the Clintons, Bill and Hillary, that is, to receive communion at a Catholic Mass they had attended. Again, political correctness above all.

Last, but not least, how to explain the disconnect between Catholic public officials, Kerry, Kennedy, Biden, Pelosi, etc., receiving the Eucharistic sacrament yet being well-known supporters of abortion, contraception, same-sex marriage, etc.? Once again it is a matter of who you are, not what you do. Enough said, the point having been belabored ad nauseam perhaps.

There are those who would blithely proclaim that laws are made to be broken, but, I submit, it reflects poorly on a Church that claims to hold the moral high ground. Gone are the days of the long confessional lines on Saturday nights as the laity has assumed more responsibility for its actions and not continued to depend solely on an all-male clergy to inflict a sense of guilt for offenses of a multi-faceted variety. The sense of sin has mutated from a laundry list of violations to a focus on cardinal weaknesses that define an individual's way of life, either toward God or against God. There is also a wide divergence as to how often the sacrament needs to be taken advantage of. My local parish suggests monthly confessions whereas another parish just a few miles away advises that twice a year might be sufficient. Perhaps the ideal lies somewhere in the middle. A priest acquaintance of mine had a novel twist on the "penance" part of the sacrament. If, for example, a married woman penitent confessed that she had sinned in some manner against her husband, he would tell her to go home and bake him a cake instead of telling her to mumble a few Our Fathers or Hail Marys. We need more confessors like that.

As to Hollywood's portrayal of the priesthood, it has come a long way from a Father O'Malley as portrayed by Bing Crosby in "Going My Way" and "The Bells of St Mary's." Now we have Father Farley as portrayed by Jack Lemmon in "Mass Appeal" or Father Fermoyle as portrayed by Tom Tryon in "The Cardinal." Priests are now presented with their foibles and warts, more in line with reality. These are flesh and blood individuals, not humanized idols to be emulated as though they were nearer to God than to man. Of course, tv got into the act with "Nothing Sacred," which was cancelled just short of its first full season due to opposition from the conservative Catholic hierarchy and laity. It was seen as too liberal by the controlling conservative bloc in the Church. Nonetheless, the toothpaste was already out of the tube, so to speak, and there was no going back to the pre-Vatican II church of the docile laity in lockstep with the controlling clergy.

Looking back over seven papacies in my lifetime I have seen the Church's ideology go from far right under Pope Pius XII to left-center under John XXIII and Paul VI and then back to far right under John Paul II and Benedict XVI. It is now trending left-center once more under Pope Francis, but this papacy, still in its early stages, has yet to show its true colors. However, due to the reforms of Vatican II, the omens augur well for more liberalization in the future, no matter how long it may take. In the final event, you cannot hold back the Spring.

Certainly the Church of my childhood and teens is not the Church of today and there is no going back in spite of the determination of the conservative element to hold the reins of authority with the tenacity of a dying breed in their cold dead hands until they have to finally give up the ghost. The center of power in the Roman Catholic Church had been centered in Europe but is now inexorably moving away from there and migrating to Latin America, Africa, and Asia. The election of a pontiff from Latin America bears testimony to that shift in evangelization. It remains now only for the Church to take the next bold step and elect a non-caucasian pope, which is an event whose time has already come and gone.

Many have argued that the Church will always exist because it has existed already for over two thousand years. This is what I would refer to as the "inertia" defense, namely, that a body once in motion tends to remain in motion just by the force of nature, but is mere existence enough. I do not doubt that the Church will continue to exist but, unless radical changes are made, e.g., married clergy, women priests, acceptance of divorced Catholics, it will not, after another generation, be the Church as we now know it. Pope John Paul II, as though aiming to rule even from beyond the grave, put in place cardinals who would continue his policies for the foreseeable future. However, after another twenty years or less, those individuals will have passed from the scene and been replaced, hopefully, by the succeeding popes with clergy more attuned to the realities of the 21st century. Ironically Pope Francis, elevated to the cardinalate by Benedict XVI, may be the first sign of the new Spring. My only regret is that I won't live to see it but I can take much consolation in knowing that others will be witnesses to it and will grow spiritually as a result.

A future generation may also experience a Vatican III with all the attendant changes that will bring, possibly paling by comparison the changes unleashed by Vatican II, which was the signature religious event of the 20th century. This time there will be no turning back of the clock as though the event could be erased from history as if it were no more than a temporary aberration or anomaly. An irreversible course will have been set and there will be no stopping it.

The Catholic Church has been a sustaining influence throughout my life and will continue to be in spite of what I see as its shortcomings and contradictions. It has made me what I am today, whatever that may be. Through daily prayers, scriptural readings and weekly Mass attendance I keep my Catholic inheritance alive. It is not as perfect as I would wish but the alternatives appear to be so much worse in the long run. What awaits me beyond the grave only God knows and, frankly, I am not in a particular hurry to find out. I have found the Church to be neither as good as I had hoped nor the outside world as wicked as it was purported to be. Sanctity knows no religious boundaries and God is most assuredly non-sectarian.

No life having at least a few regrets, I refuse to dwell on mine or speculate about the road not taken. On the contrary, I have always had the feeling that events, more often than not, worked to my advantage.

Whether this was pure luck or divine intervention or even a combination of both, only God knows. When misfortune inevitably came my way I always somehow managed to not only survive it but also to learn and grow stronger as a result. My final wish is to be at peace with myself and if writing this book in any way helps to achieve that goal then it would have been well worth the effort. It will serve as its own reward in that it will be a permanent record of my life's journey from the womb to the tomb. It is a journey, I submit, that could not have been completed without my foundation in the regimen of the Roman Catholic Church. I would not have had it any other way.

Epilogue

On entering many Catholic churches today, none more so than my current parish of St. William of York in Stafford, Virginia, one has the distinct impression of going through a time warp back into the mid-20th century. At my parish Latin inscriptions adorn the main altar, the sacrament of Reconciliation is referred to as "Penance," homilies rage against the intrinsic evil of contraception, and no deviation from ritualistic procedures is permitted. A Latin Mass is also offered once a week. The hierarchy, the vaunted magisterium, is the sole and final arbiter of all things Catholic.

What once promised to be a reawakening and rejuvenation of Catholic spirituality in a modern embrace of rapport and fellowship, not only among Catholics but between Christians, commonly referred to as ecumenism, has turned into a retrenchment embracing past divisions and ideologies. The window good Pope John opened to let in a breath of fresh air has been slammed shut, leaving a dank and musty odor in its wake. Twenty years of progressive religious activity has been replaced by, to date, thirty-six years of movement forward into the past. What promised to be a new beginning under the papacies of John XXIII and Paul VI has been systematically undermined by the ensuing reigns of John Paul II and Benedict XVI. The tragic papacy of John Paul I, offering even greater hope, died aborning. It was most fitting that Albino Luciani took the name John Paul I as an affirmation of his intention to continue and fulfill the legacies of his two immediate predecessors. Following his untimely death and the election of Karol Wojtyla, his fellow cardinals insisted that he take up the cudgels, so to speak, and take upon himself the appellation of his short-lived predecessor, thus becoming John Paul II. In the event, this turned out to be a cruel charade indeed as he had no real intention of following in his predecessors' footsteps, but, rather, was intent upon a new beginning, signified by his spoken desire to be known as Stanislaus I. At least this would have been a true barometer of his papal intentions, rather than a duplicitous implication that he was going to pursue the agendas of the three preceding papacies. As we learned all too soon and, I submit, to our great chagrin, nothing could have been further from the truth.

John Paul II started his purge of dissidents before he could even warm St. Peter's chair with his corralling of the Lefebvrists. Clergy and laity alike would soon learn that here was irrefutable proof that what you saw was not what you would get. Charisma, however, can take you only so far and people quickly found they liked the messenger but not the message. This was, sadly, only a harbinger of things to come. Women quickly found they were still to be regarded as second-class believers and can kindly take their seats, thank you, at the back of the bus. After the failed assassination attempt on John Paul II in1981, the parody only intensified as the Pope credited his escape from death to the miraculous intercession of Mary, the Mother of God. In reality there is a much more mundane reason, namely, the last-second intervention by a nun who jolted the assassin's arm as he was taking aim. So, in the event, a woman did very probably save John Paul's life, but it was an earthly, not a heavenly, one. Mary ironically became a surrogate mother for the Pole, who apparently felt betrayed by his earthly mother who died while he was still young. Other women were seen as objects to be kept in their place by this uncompassionate, misogynistic ideologue. The issue of women priests was not only not to be discussed but also forever forbidden as even a possibility. Eventually, insult was added to injury, if you will, by his successor's attempt to define such an action as comparable to the ongoing sexual abuse crisis. In a continuing cleansing of dissent, theologians such as Bernard Haring, Edward Schillebeeckx, Hans Kung, Charles Curran, and Karl Rahner were quickly put on notice that their deviations from the party line would no longer be tolerated. In their place, John Paul appointed ecclesiastical mental midgets as his minions who would undeviatingly follow his dictates not only while he was alive but even long after he was gone. If John Paul were more concerned about the church's welfare than we was about his papal perogatives, he would have had the decency to vacate his office in 2000, a landmark moment in church as well as secular history. Instead he lingered on for another long, torturous five years during which power was increasingly ceded to his right-hand man, Cardinal Joseph Ratzinger, and to the Curia. The subsequent succession of Ratzinger to the papacy was not so much an election as it was, I submit, a passing of the fisherman's ring. Benedict XVI has proceeded to preside over the legacy of his predecessor with but a few exceptions. He has, to his everlasting credit, confronted the sexual abuse crisis and attempted to exert damage control. A firmer hand on the debacle has been exerted, as witness his handling of the Marcial Maciel affair. In reaching out to Lutheran clergy he has attempted to revive at least a semblance of ecumenism. You could not expect monumental moves by a papacy universally considered and expected to be transitional, as it ultimately was.

Most contradictorally, the Catholic Church has always repeated the Marian mantra of its devotion and exaltation of the Mother of God, as in the Legion of Mary, novenas to Mary, sodalities, etc., all the while diminishing the role of women not only within but outside the church as well. The role of deacon has been revived but not that of deaconess. Women religious orders, having tasted a fresh air of freedom post Vatican II, have been summarily thrust back into their role as subservient to the clergy. Through a McCarthyistic examination of their adherence to hierarchical diktats, euphemistically referred to as "apostolic visitations," they have been warned that no deviation from Vatican pronouncements will be entertained. Outside the religious framework, no deviance from the omnipotent magisterium will be tolerated, whether it be in regard to birth control, abortion, or divorce. Women must be kept subordinate to men in all matters spiritual as well as physical. How ironic it is that, if there were women priests, we might quite possibly never have had a scandal of sexual abuse. Did not Pentecost tell us anything? Among the apostles, confirmed in a most miraculous way by the Holy Spirit, stood the Mother of God. Were not all of these anointed souls sent forth to spread the word of the gospel, Mary included? To admit this would be to reveal the Church's dirty little secret that Mary, in effect, was the first woman priest. Heaven forbid!

The Catholic Church prides itself on its over one billion membership, but there is a vast chasm between membership and participation. It is conservatively estimated that one in ten American Catholics has left the Church, comprising what would be the second largest denomination in the U.S. if it were to be classified as such. Attendance at Mass in the U.S. is considered to be even below fifty percent of those registered as practicing Catholics. In Europe as well, not to mention in the Pope's own country, attendance has dropped to record lows. The Catholic Church now looks to spread its message to the peripheries of its missionary pursuits in Asia and Africa, having lost its stronghold in Europe. Moreover, beleaguered by sexual scandals worldwide, it has suffered severe financial setbacks, particularly in the U.S., where several dioceses have already declared bankruptcy, churches have been closed and consolidated, and schools have been shuttered. The Vatican claims fiscal solvency after several years of being in the red, but it is experiencing nothing like the financial prosperity it enjoyed during the halcyon days of the reign of Pope Pius XII. Vatican bank improprieties continue to resurface periodically even under the current pontificate.

If the prophecies of Malachi are to be believed, the next papacy will be the last and, supposedly, a more traditionally extended one, not to mention one of apocalyptic and cataclysmic proportions. In its present state and according to Christ's promise that the Church would survive until the end of time, one must wonder if the hierarchy might be wishing that the second coming will not be long in coming, so to speak. The Catholic Church cannot wait for another Vatican Council with the leadership of a John XXIII to set it aright, unless the frequency of such councils is considerably abridged. It was almost 100 years between the first and second Vatican Councils. By the time such a council would materialize, if it ever did, one has to wonder how many people, especially Catholics, would even care.

CPSIA information can be obtained at www.ICGtesting.com
Printed in the USA
LVOW10s2103210715

447060LV00001B/305/P